Assessing National
Achievement
Levels in
Education

National Assessments of Educational Achievement

VOLUME 1

Assessing National Achievement Levels in Education

Vincent Greaney
Thomas Kellaghan

 THE WORLD BANK

Cover design: Naylor Design, Washington, DC

ISBN-13: 978-0-8213-7258-6
eISBN: 978-0-8213-7259-3
DOI: 1596/978-0-8213-7258-6

Library of Congress Cataloging-in-Publication Data
Assessing national achievement levels in education / [edited by] Vincent Greaney and Thomas Kellaghan.
    p. cm.
Includes bibliographical references.
ISBN 978-0-8213-7258-6 (alk. paper) — ISBN 978-0-8213-7259-3
1. Educational tests and measurements. 2. Educational evaluation. I. Greaney, Vincent. II. Kellaghan, Thomas.
LB3051.A7663 2007
371.26'2—dc22
2007022161

CONTENTS

BOXES

FIGURES

TABLES

PREFACE

In a speech to mark the first 100 days of his presidency of the World Bank Group, Robert Zoellick outlined six strategic themes to guide the Bank's work in promoting an inclusive and sustainable globalization. One of those themes focused on the role of the Bank as "a unique and special institution of knowledge and learning.... a brain trust of applied experience." Zoellick noted that this role requires the Bank "to focus continually and rigorously on results and on the assessment of effectiveness."

This challenge is greatest in education, where the large body of empirical evidence linking education to economic growth indicates that improved enrollment and completion rates are necessary, but not sufficient, conditions for poverty reduction. Instead, enhanced learning outcomes—in the form of increased student knowledge and cognitive skills—are key to alleviating poverty and improving economic competitiveness (and will be crucial for sustaining the gains achieved in education access to date). In other words, the full potency of education in relation to economic growth can only be realized if the education on offer is of high quality and student knowledge and cognitive skills are developed.

The available evidence indicates that the quality of learning outcomes in developing countries is very poor. At the same time, few of these countries systematically monitor such outcomes either through conducting their own assessments of student achievement or through participating in regional or international assessments. The lack of this type of regular, system-level information on student learning makes it difficult to gauge overall levels of achievement, to assess the relative performance of particular subgroups, and to monitor changes in performance over time. It also makes it difficult to determine the effectiveness of government policies designed to improve outcomes in these and other areas.

This is a core issue for the Bank and its client countries as the focus shifts from access to achievement. It also is an area in which there is a dearth of tools and resources suited to the needs of developing countries. This series of books, edited by Vincent Greaney and Thomas Kellaghan, contributes in a significant way to closing this gap. The series is designed to address many of the issues involved in making learning outcomes a more central part of the educational agenda in lower-income countries. It will help countries to develop capacity to measure national levels of student learning in more valid, sustainable, and systematic ways. Such capacity will hopefully translate into evidence-based policymaking that leads to observable improvement in the quality of student learning. It is an important building block toward achieving the real promise of education for dynamic economies.

Marguerite Clarke
Senior Education Specialist
The World Bank

ACKNOWLEDGMENTS

A team led by Vincent Greaney (consultant, Human Development Network, Education Group, World Bank) and Thomas Kellaghan (Educational Research Centre, St. Patrick's College, Dublin) prepared this series of books.

Other contributors to the series were Sylvia Acana (Uganda National Examinations Board), Prue Anderson (Australian Council for Educational Research), Fernando Cartwright (Canadian Council on Learning), Jean Dumais (Statistics Canada), Chris Freeman (Australian Council for Educational Research), Hew Gough (Statistics Canada), Sara Howie (University of Pretoria), George Morgan (Australian Council for Educational Research), T. Scott Murray (DataAngel Policy Research) and Gerry Shiel (Educational Research Centre, St. Patrick's College, Dublin).

The work was carried out under the general direction of Ruth Kagia, World Bank Education Sector Director, and Robin Horn, Education Sector Manager. Robert Prouty initiated and supervised the project up to August 2007. Marguerite Clarke supervised the project in its later stages through review and publication. We are grateful for contributions of the review panel: Al Beaton (Boston College), Irwin Kirsch (Educational Testing Service), and Benoit Millot (World Bank).

Additional peer-review comments were provided by a number of World Bank staff, including Carlos Rojas, Eduardo Velez, Elizabeth King, Harry Patrinos, Helen Abadzi, Jee-Peng Tan, Marguerite Clarke, Maureen Lewis, Raisa Venalainen, Regina Bendokat, Robert Prouty, and Robin Horn.

Special thanks are due to Aidan Mulkeen and to Sarah Plouffe. We received valuable support from Cynthia Guttman, Matseko Ramokoena, Aleksandra Sawicka, Pam Spagnoli, Beata Thorstensen, Myriam Waiser, Peter Winograd, and Hans Wagemaker. We are also grateful to Patricia Arregui, Harsha Aturupane, Luis Benveniste, Jean-Marc Bernard, Carly Cheevers, Zewdu Gebrekidan, Venita Kaul, Pedro Ravela, and Kin Bing Wu.

We wish to thank the following institutions for permission to reproduce material: Examinations Council of Lesotho, International Association for the Evaluation of Educational Achievement, National Center for Education Statistics of the U.S. Department of Education, the Organisation for Economic Co-operation and Development, and the Papua New Guinea Department of Education.

Hilary Walshe helped prepare the manuscript. Book design, editing, and production were coordinated by Mary Fisk and Paola Scalabrin of the World Bank's Office of the Publisher.

The Irish Educational Trust Fund; the Bank Netherlands Partnership Program; the Educational Research Centre, Dublin; and the Australian Council for Educational Research have generously supported preparation and publication of this series.

ABBREVIATIONS

CONFEMEN	Conférence des Ministres de l'Education des Pays ayant le Français en Partage
DiNIECE	Dirección Nacional de Información y Evaluación de la Calidad Educativa (Argentina)
EFA	Education for All
IEA	International Association for the Evaluation of Educational Achievement
IIEP	International Institute for Educational Planning
LLECE	Laboratorio Latinoamericano de Evaluación de la Calidad de la Educación
MOE	ministry of education
MESyFOD	Modernización de la Educación Secundaria y Formación Docente (Uruguay)
NAEP	National Assessment of Educational Progress (United States)
NAPE	National Assessment of Progress in Education (Uganda)
NSC	national steering committee
OECD	Organisation for Economic Co-operation and Development
PASEC	Programme d'Analyse des Systèmes Éducatifs de la CONFEMEN
PIRLS	Progress in International Reading Literacy Study

PISA   Programme for International Student Assessment
SACMEQ   Southern and Eastern Africa Consortium for
            Monitoring Educational Quality
SIMCE   Sistema de Medición de la Calidad de la Educación
            (Chile)
SNED   National System of Teacher Performance Assess-
            ment in Publicly Supported Schools (Chile)
SSA   Sarva Shiksha Abhiyan (India)
TA   technical assistance
TIMSS   Trends in International Mathematics and Science
            Study
UMRE   Unidad de Medición de Resultados Educativos
            (Uruguay)
UNEB   Uganda National Examinations Board
UNESCO   United Nations Educational, Scientific, and Cul-
            tural Organization

CHAPTER 1

INTRODUCTION

In this introductory book, we describe the main features of national and international assessments, both of which became extremely popular tools for determining the quality of education in the 1990s and 2000s. This increase in popularity reflects two important developments. First, it reflects increasing globalization and interest in global mandates, including Education for All (UNESCO 2000). Second, it represents an overall shift in emphasis in assessing the quality of education from a concern with inputs (such as student participation rates, physical facilities, curriculum materials, and teacher training) to a concern with outcomes (such as the knowledge and skills that students have acquired as a result of their exposure to schooling) (Kellaghan and Greaney 2001b). This emphasis on outcomes can, in turn, be considered an expression of concern with the development of human capital in the belief (a) that knowledge is replacing raw materials and labor as resources in economic development and (b) that the availability of human knowledge and skills is critical in determining a country's rate of economic development and its competitiveness in an international market (Kellaghan and Greaney 2001a). A response to this concern has required information on the performance of education systems, which, in turn, has involved a shift from the traditional use of achievement tests to assess individual students toward their use to obtain information about the achievements of the system of education as a whole (or a clearly defined part of the system).

The development of national assessment capacity has enabled ministries of education—as part of their management function—to describe national levels of learning achievement, especially in key subject areas, and to compare achievement levels of key subgroups (such as boys and girls, ethnic groups, urban and rural students, and public and private school students). It has also provided evidence that enables ministries to support or refute claims that standards of student achievement are rising or falling over time.

Despite growth in national and international assessment activity, a lack of appreciation still exists in many quarters about the potential value of the data that assessments can provide, as well as a deficit in the skills required to carry out a technically sound assessment. Even when countries conduct a national assessment or participate in an international one, the information yielded by the assessment is frequently not fully exploited. A number of reasons may account for this: the policy makers may have been only peripherally involved in the assessment and may not have been fully committed to it; the results of analyses may not have been communicated in a form that was intelligible to policy makers; or the policy makers may not have fully appreciated the implications of findings for social policy in general or for educational policy in particular relating to curricular provision, the allocation of resources, the practice of teaching, and teachers' professional development.

This series of books is designed to address such issues by introducing readers to the complex technology that has grown up around the administration of national and international assessments. This introductory book describes key national assessment concepts and procedures. It is intended primarily for policy makers and decision makers in education. The purposes and main features of *national assessments* are described in chapter 2 (see also appendix A). The reasons for carrying out a national assessment are considered in chapter 3, and the main decisions that have to be made in the design and planning of an assessment are covered in chapter 4. Issues (as well as common errors) to be borne in mind in the design, implementation, analysis, reporting, and use of a national assessment are identified in chapter 5. In chapter 6, *international assessments* of student achievement, which share many procedural features with national assessments (such as sampling, administration, background data collected, and methods of analysis—see appendix B), are described.

The main point of difference between national and international assessments highlights both a strength and a weakness of an international assessment. The strength is that an international assessment provides data from a number of countries, thereby allowing each country to compare the results of its students with the results achieved by students in other countries. The weakness is that the requirement that test instruments be acceptable in all participating countries means that they may not accurately reflect the range of achievements of students in individual countries.

A further feature of international assessments is that many participating countries carry out internal analyses that are based on data collected within a country. Thus, the data collected for the international study can be used for what is, in effect, a national assessment. However, the practice is not without its problems, and the data that are collected in this way may be less appropriate for policy than if they had been collected for a dedicated national assessment.

An intermediate procedure that lies between national assessments in individual countries and large-scale international studies that span the globe is the *regional study* in which a number of countries in a region that may share many socioeconomic and cultural features collaborate in a study (see appendix C).

A further variation is a *subnational assessment* in which an assessment is confined to a region (a province or state) within a country. Subnational assessments have been carried out in a number of large countries (such as Argentina, Brazil, and the United States) to meet local or regional information needs. Those exercises are relatively independent and differ from national assessments in that participants in all regions within a country do not respond to the same instruments and procedures; thus, direct comparisons of student achievement between regions are not possible.

In the final chapter of this volume, some overall conclusions are presented, together with consideration of conditions relating to the development and institutionalization of national assessment capacity and to the optimal use of assessment findings. At the end of the book, the main features of national assessments in nine countries are described (appendix A), followed by descriptions of three international studies (appendix B) and three regional studies (appendix C).

Subsequent books in this series provide details of the design and implementation of a national assessment. The books are designed to provide those directly involved in the tasks of constructing tests and questionnaires and of collecting, analyzing, or describing data in a national assessment with an introduction to—and basic skills in—key technical aspects of the tasks involved.

The second book, *Developing Tests and Questionnaires for a National Assessment of Educational Achievement*, has sections on developing (a) achievement tests, (b) questionnaires, and (c) administration manuals. The first section addresses the design of achievement tests and the role that a test framework and blueprint or table of specifications plays in the design. It describes the process of item writing and gives examples of various item types, including multiple-choice, short-answer, and open-ended response items. It also describes the item review or paneling process, an essential exercise to ensure test-content validity. It includes guidelines for conducting pretests, selecting items for the final test, and producing the final version of a test. The section concludes with a brief treatment of training scorers or raters and hand-scoring test items. The second section describes steps in the construction of questionnaires: designing a questionnaire, writing items, scoring and coding responses, and linking data derived from the questionnaire with students' achievement scores. The final section describes the design and content of an administration manual and the selection and role of a test administrator. The book has an accompanying CD, which contains test and questionnaire items released from national and international assessments and a test administration manual.

Implementing a National Assessment of Educational Achievement, the third book in the series, is also divided into three sections. The first section focuses on practical issues to be addressed in implementing a large-scale national assessment program. It covers planning, budgeting, staffing, arranging facilities and equipment, contacting schools, selecting test administrators, packing and shipping, and ensuring test security. This section also covers the logistical aspects of test scoring, data cleaning, and report writing. The second section includes a step-by-step guide designed to enable assessment teams to draw an appropriate national sample. It includes a CD with sampling software and a training dataset to be used in conjunction with the guide. Topics addressed are defining the population to be assessed, creating a sampling frame, calculating an appropriate sample size, sampling with probability proportional to size, and conducting multistage sampling. Data cleaning and data management are treated in the final section. This section is also supported by a CD with step-by-step exercises to help users prepare national assessment data for analysis. Procedures for data verification and data validation, including "wild codes" and within-file and between-file consistency checks, are described.

Analyzing Data from a National Assessment of Educational Achievement, the fourth book, is supported by two CDs, which require users to apply statistical procedures to datasets and to check their mastery levels against solutions depicted on screenshots in the text. The first half of the book deals with the generation of item-level data using both classical test and item response theory approaches. Topics addressed include analyzing pilot and final test items, monitoring change in performance over time, building a test from previously created items, equating, and developing performance or proficiency levels. The second half of the book is designed to help analysts carry out basic-level analysis of national assessment results and includes sections on measures of central tendency and dispersion, mean score differences, identification of high and low achievers, correlation, regression, and visual representation of data.

Reporting and Using Results from a National Assessment of Educational Achievement, the final book in the series, focuses on writing reports in a way that will influence policy. It introduces a methodology for designing a dissemination and communication strategy for a national assessment program. It also describes the preparation of a technical report, press releases, briefings for key policy makers, and reports for teachers and other specialist groups. The second section of the book highlights ways that countries have actually used the results of national assessments for policy making, curriculum reform, resource allocation, teacher training, accountability, and monitoring of changes in achievement and other variables over time.

Those who study the content of these books and who carry out the specified exercises should acquire the basic skills required for a national assessment. They should, however, bear in mind three factors. First, they should not regard the books as providing simple formulas or algorithms to be applied mechanically but should be prepared to exercise judgment at varying points in the national assessment (for example, in selection of test content, in sampling, and in analysis). Judgment in these matters should improve with experience. Second, users may, on occasion, require the advice of more experienced practitioners in making their judgments. Third, users should be prepared to adapt to the changes in knowledge and technology that will inevitably occur in the coming years.

NATIONAL ASSESSMENTS OF STUDENT ACHIEVEMENT

We begin the chapter by defining a national assessment and listing questions that a national assessment would be designed to answer. A listing of the main elements of a national assessment follows. Finally, we consider the differences between a national assessment and public examinations.

A national assessment is designed to describe the achievement of students in a curriculum area aggregated to provide an estimate of the achievement level in the education system as a whole at a particular age or grade level. It provides data for a type of national education audit carried out to inform policy makers about key aspects of the system. Normally, it involves administration of achievement tests either to a sample or to a population of students, usually focusing on a particular sector in the system (such as fifth grade or 13-year-old students). Teachers and others (for example, parents, principals, and students) may be asked to provide background information, usually in questionnaires, which, when related to student achievement, can provide insights about how achievement is related to factors such as household characteristics, levels of teacher training, teachers' attitudes toward curriculum areas, teacher knowledge, and availability of teaching and learning materials.

National assessment systems in various parts of the world tend to have common features. All include an assessment of students' language or literacy and of students' mathematics abilities or numeracy. Some systems assess students' achievements in a second language, science, art, music, or social studies. In practically all national assessment systems, students at the primary-school level are assessed. In many systems, national assessments are also carried out in secondary school, usually during the period of compulsory education.

Differences also exist in national assessment systems from country to country. First, they differ in the frequency with which assessments are carried out. In some countries, an assessment is carried out every year, although the curriculum area that is assessed may vary from year to year. In other systems, assessments are less frequent. Second, they differ in the agency that carries out an assessment. In some systems, the ministry of education carries out the assessment; in others, the assessment is by a national research center, a consortium of educational bodies, a university, or an examination board. Third, participation by a school may be voluntary or may be mandated. When voluntary, nonparticipation of some schools will almost invariably bias the results and lead to an inaccurate reflection of achievement levels in the education system.

Although most industrial countries have had systems of national assessment for some time, it was not until the 1990s that the capacity to administer assessments became more widely available in other parts of the world. For example, rapid development in the establishment of national assessments took place during the 1990s in Latin American and Caribbean counties, often to provide baseline data for educational reforms (Rojas and Esquivel 1998). The development represented a shift in the assessment of quality from emphasis on educational inputs to outcomes following the Jomtien Declaration (see *World Declaration on Education for All* 1990). Article 4 of the Jomtien Declaration states that the focus of basic education should be "on actual learning acquisition and outcome, rather than exclusively upon enrolment, continued participation in organized programs and completion of certification requirements" (*World Declaration on Education for All* 1990, 5). More recently, the Dakar Framework for Action (UNESCO 2000), which was produced at the end of the 10-year follow-up to Jomtien, again highlighted the importance of learning outcomes. Among its list of seven agreed goals was, by 2015, to improve "all aspects of the quality of education ... so that recognised and measurable outcomes are achieved by all, especially in literacy, numeracy, and essential life skills" (UNESCO 2000, iv, 7).

These statements imply that, for countries pledged to achieving the goals of Education for All (EFA), efforts to enhance the quality of education will have to be accompanied by procedures that will provide information on students' learning. As a result, national governments and donor agencies have greatly increased support for monitoring student achievement through national assessments. The assumption is frequently made not only that national assessments will provide information on the state of education, but also that use of the information should lead to improvement in student achievements. Whether this improvement ultimately happens remains to be seen. So far, the expectation that EFA and regular monitoring of achievement levels would result in an improvement in learning standards does not seem to have materialized (Postlethwaite 2004). This outcome may be because—although EFA led to rapid increases in numbers attending school—larger numbers were not matched by increased resources (especially trained teachers). Furthermore, the information obtained from assessments has often been of poor quality, and even when it has not, it has not been systematically factored into decision making.

All national assessments seek answers to one or more of the following questions:

- How well are students learning in the education system (with reference to general expectations, aims of the curriculum, preparation for further learning, or preparation for life)?
- Does evidence indicate particular strengths and weaknesses in students' knowledge and skills?
- Do particular subgroups in the population perform poorly? Do disparities exist, for example, between the achievements of (a) boys and girls, (b) students in urban and rural locations, (c) students from different language or ethnic groups, or (d) students in different regions of the country?
- What factors are associated with student achievement? To what extent does achievement vary with characteristics of the learning

environment (for example, school resources, teacher preparation and competence, and type of school) or with students' home and community circumstances?

- Are government standards being met in the provision of resources (for example, textbooks, teacher qualifications, and other quality inputs)?
- Do the achievements of students change over time? This question may be of particular interest if reforms of the education system are being undertaken. Answering the question requires carrying out assessments that yield comparable data at different points in time (Kellaghan and Greaney 2001b, 2004).

Most of those questions were addressed in the design and implementation of Ethiopia's national assessment (see box 2.1).

A feature of Vietnam's approach to national assessment, in addition to assessing student achievement, was a strong focus on key inputs, such as physical conditions in schools, access to educational materials, and teacher qualifications (see box 2.2).

BOX 2.1

Ethiopia: National Assessment Objectives

1. To determine the level of student academic achievement and attitude development in Ethiopian primary education.

2. To analyze variations in student achievement by region, gender, location, and language of instruction.

3. To explore factors that influence student achievement in primary education.

4. To monitor the improvement of student learning achievement from the first baseline study in 1999/2000.

5. To build the capacity of the education system in national assessment.

6. To create reliable baseline data for the future.

7. To generate recommendations for policy making to improve educational quality.

Source: Ethiopia, National Organisation for Examinations 2005.

BOX 2.2

Example of Questions Addressed by Vietnam's National Assessment

Questions Related to Inputs

- What are the characteristics of grade 5 pupils?
- What are the teaching conditions in grade 5 classrooms and in primary schools?
- What is the general condition of the school buildings?

Questions Related to Standards of Educational Provision

- Were ministry standards met regarding
  - Class size?
  - Classroom furniture?
  - Qualifications of staff members?

Questions Related to Equity of School Inputs

- Was there equity of resources among provinces and among schools within provinces in terms of
  - Material resource inputs?
  - Human resource inputs?

Questions Related to Achievement

- What percentage of pupils reached the different levels of skills in reading and mathematics?
- What was the level of grade 5 teachers in reading and mathematics?

Questions Related to Influences on Achievement

- What were the major factors accounting for the variance in reading and mathematics achievement?
- What were the major variables that differentiated between the most and least effective schools?

Source: World Bank 2004.

WHAT ARE THE MAIN ELEMENTS IN A NATIONAL ASSESSMENT?

Although national assessments can vary in how they are implemented, they tend to have a number of common elements (see box 2.3 and Kellaghan and Greaney 2001b, 2004).

BOX 2.3

Main Elements of a National Assessment

- The ministry of education (MOE) appoints either an implementing agency within the ministry or an independent external body (for example, a university department or a research organization), and it provides funding.

- The MOE determines policy needs to be addressed in the assessment, sometimes in consultation with key education stakeholders (for example, teachers' representatives, curriculum specialists, business people, and parents).

- The MOE, or a steering committee nominated by it, identifies the population to be assessed (for example, fourth grade students).

- The MOE determines the area of achievement to be assessed (for example, literacy or numeracy).

- The implementing agency defines the area of achievement and describes it in terms of content and cognitive skills.

- The implementing agency prepares achievement tests and supporting questionnaires and administration manuals, and it takes steps to ensure their validity.

- The tests and supporting documents are pilot-tested by the implementing agency and subsequently are reviewed by the steering committee and other competent bodies to (a) determine curriculum appropriateness and (b) ensure that items reflect gender, ethnic, and cultural sensitivities.

- The implementing agency selects the targeted sample (or population) of schools or students, arranges for printing of materials, and establishes communication with selected schools.

- The implementing agency trains test administrators (for example, classroom teachers, school inspectors, or graduate university students).

- The survey instruments (tests and questionnaires) are administered in schools on a specified date under the overall direction of the implementing agency.

- The implementing agency takes responsibility for collecting survey instruments, for scoring, and for cleaning and preparing data for analysis.

(continued)

BOX 2.3

- The implementing agency establishes the reliability of the assessment instruments and procedures.

- The implementing agency carries out the data analysis.

- The draft reports are prepared by the implementing agency and reviewed by the steering committee.

- The final reports are prepared by the implementing agency and are disseminated by the appropriate authority.

- The MOE and other relevant stakeholders review the results in light of the policy needs that they are meant to address and determine an appropriate course of action.

Source: Authors.

It is clear from the list of elements in box 2.3 that a good deal of thought and preparation are required before students respond to assessment tasks. A body with responsibility for collecting data must be appointed, decisions must be made about the policy issues to be addressed, and tests and questionnaires must be designed and tried out. In preparation for the actual testing, samples (or populations) of schools and of students must be identified, schools must be contacted, and test administrators must be selected and trained. In some countries (for example, India, Vietnam, and some African countries), teachers have been assessed on the tasks taken by their students (see A.1 and A.2 in appendix A and C.1 in appendix C). Following test administration, a lot of time and effort will be required to prepare data for analysis, to carry out analyses, and to write reports.

Low-income countries have to deal with problems over and above those encountered by other countries in attempting to carry out a national assessment. Education budgets may be meager. According to 2005 data (World Bank 2007), some countries devote 2 percent or less of gross domestic product to public education (for example, Bangladesh, Cameroon, Chad, the Dominican Republic, Guinea, Kazakhstan, the Lao People's Democratic Republic, Mauritania, Pakistan, Peru, the Republic of Congo, United Arab Emirates, and Zambia) compared to more than 5 percent in most middle- and high-income countries.

Competing demands within the education sector for activities such as school construction, teacher training, and provision of educational materials can result in nonavailability of funds for monitoring educational achievement. Furthermore, many low- and, indeed, middle-income countries have weak institutional capacity for carrying out a national assessment. They may also have to face additional administrative and communication problems caused by inadequate roads, mail service, and telephone service. Finally, the very high between-school variation in student achievement found in some low-income countries requires a large sample (see UNEB 2006; World Bank 2004).

HOW DOES A NATIONAL ASSESSMENT DIFFER FROM PUBLIC EXAMINATIONS?

Public examinations play a crucial role in many education systems in certifying student achievement, in selecting students for further study, and in standardizing what is taught and learned in schools. Sometimes, public examinations are thought to provide the same information as a national assessment, thus appearing to eliminate the need for a national assessment system in a country that has a public examination system. However, public examinations cannot provide the kind of information that a national assessment seeks to provide.

First, since public examinations play a major role in selecting students (for the next highest level in the education system and sometimes for jobs), they seek to discriminate between relatively high achieving students and so may not provide adequate coverage of the curriculum. Second, examinations, as well as the characteristics of students who take them, change from year to year, thereby limiting the inferences that can be made from comparisons over time. Third, the fact that "high stakes" are attached to performance (that is, how students do on an examination has important consequences for them and perhaps for their teachers) means that teachers (and students) may focus on those areas of the curriculum that are examined to the neglect of important areas that are not examined (for example, practical skills), so that performance on the examination does not provide

TABLE 2.1

Differences between National Assessments and Public Examinations

	National assessments	Public examinations
Purpose	To provide feedback to policy makers.	To certify and select students.
Frequency	For individual subjects offered on a regular basis (such as every four years).	Annually and more often where the system allows for repeats.
Duration	One or two days.	Can extend over a few weeks.
Who is tested?	Usually a sample of students at a particular grade or age level.	All students who wish to take this examination at the examination grade level.
Format	Usually multiple choice and short answer.	Usually essay and multiple choice.
Stakes: importance for students, teachers, and others	Low importance.	Great importance.
Coverage of curriculum	Generally confined to one or two subjects.	Covers main subject areas.
Effect on teaching	Very little direct effect.	Major effect: teacher tendency to teach what is expected on the examination.
Additional tuition sought for students	Very unlikely.	Frequently.
Do students get results?	Seldom.	Yes.
Is additional information collected from students?	Frequently, in student questionnaires.	Seldom.
Scoring	Usually involves statistically sophisticated techniques.	Usually a simple process that is based on a predetermined marking scheme.
Effect on level of student attainment	Unlikely to have an effect.	Poor results or the prospect of failure, which can lead to early dropout.
Usefulness for monitoring trends in achievement levels over time	Appropriate if tests are designed with monitoring in mind.	Not appropriate because examination questions and candidate populations change from year to year.

Source: Authors.

an accurate reflection of the intended curriculum. Although there are some exceptions, decisions about individual students, teachers, or schools are not normally made following a national assessment.

Fourth, information on student achievement is usually required at an earlier age than that at which public examinations are held. Fifth, the kind of contextual information (about teaching, resources, and students and their homes) that is used in the interpretation of achievement data collected in national assessments is not available to interpret public examination results (Kellaghan 2006). Table 2.1 summarizes the major differences between national assessments and public examinations.

CHAPTER 3

WHY CARRY OUT
A NATIONAL
ASSESSMENT?

A decision to carry out a national assessment might be made for a variety of reasons. Frequently, national assessments reflect the efforts of a government to "modernize" its education system by introducing a business management (corporatist) approach (Kellaghan 2003). This approach draws on concepts used in the world of business, such as strategic planning and a focus on deliverables and results, and it may involve accountability based on performance. Viewed from this perspective, a national assessment is a tool for providing feedback on a limited number of outcome measures that are considered important by policy makers, politicians, and the broader educational community.

A key objective of this approach is to provide information on the operation of the education system. Many governments lack basic information on aspects of the system—especially student achievement levels—and even on basic inputs to the system. National assessments can provide such information, which is a key prerequisite for sound policy making. For example, Vietnam's national assessment helped establish that many classrooms lacked basic resources (World Bank 2004). In a similar vein, Zanzibar's assessment reported that 45 percent of pupils lacked a place to sit (Nassor and Mohammed 1998). Bhutan's national assessment noted that some students had to spend several hours each day traveling to and from school (Bhutan, Board of Examinations, Ministry of Education 2004). Namibia's assessment showed that many teachers had limited mastery of basic skills in English and mathematics (Makuwa 2005).

The need to obtain information on what students learn at school has assumed increasing importance with the development of the so-called knowledge economy. Some analysts argue that students will need higher levels of knowledge and skills—particularly in the areas of mathematics and science—than in the past if they are to participate meaningfully in the world of work in the future. Furthermore, because ready access to goods and services increases with globalization, a country's ability to compete successfully is considered to depend to a considerable degree on the skills of workers and management in their use of capital and technology. This factor might point to the need to compare the performance of students in one's education system with the performance of students in other systems, although a danger exists in assigning too much importance to aggregate student achievement in accounting for economic growth, given the many other factors involved (Kellaghan and Greaney 2001a).

National assessments, when administered over a period of time, can be used to determine whether standards improve, deteriorate, or remain static. Many developing countries face the problem of expanding enrollments, building many new schools, and training large numbers of teachers while at the same time trying to improve the quality of education—sometimes against a background of a decreased budget. In this situation, governments need to monitor achievement levels to determine how changes in enrollment and budgetary conditions affect the quality of learning. Otherwise, the risk exists that increased enrollment rates may be readily accepted as evidence of an improvement in the quality of education.

National assessment data have been used to monitor achievement over time. A series of studies in Africa between 1995/96 and 2000/01 revealed a significant decline in reading literacy scores in Malawi, Namibia, and Zambia (see figure C.1.2 in appendix C). In the United States, the National Assessment of Educational Progress (NAEP), which has monitored levels of reading achievement over almost three decades, found that although nine-year-old black and Hispanic children reduced the achievement gap with whites up to about 1980, the test score differential remained fairly constant thereafter (figure 3.1). Also in the United States, the NAEP helped identify the changing levels of reading achievement in various states (figure 3.2). In Nepal, results of national assessments were used to monitor (a) changes in achievement over the period 1997–2001 and, in particular, (b) effects of policy decisions relating to budget, curricula, textbooks, teaching materials, and teacher development (see A.6 in appendix A).

When national assessment data are used to monitor achievement over time, the same test should be used in each assessment or, if different tests are used, some items should be common, so that performance on the tests can be equated or linked. In either case, the common items should be kept secure so that student or teacher familiarity with their content does not invalidate the comparisons being made.

Other uses that can be made of a national assessment depend on whether data were collected in a sample of schools or in a census in which information is obtained about all (or most) schools. In both cases, results can be used to provide direction to policy makers who are interested in enhancing educational quality. For example, the results can help governments identify the strength of the association between the quality of student learning and various factors over which they have some control (for example, availability of textbooks, class size, and number of years of teacher preservice training).

FIGURE 3.1

The Achievement Gap in the United States for Nine-Year-Old Students: NAEP Reading Assessment, 1971–99

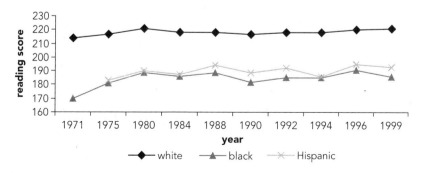

Source: Winograd and Thorstensen 2004.

FIGURE 3.2

Percentages of Fourth Grade Students at or above "Proficient" in Reading, NAEP 1992–2003

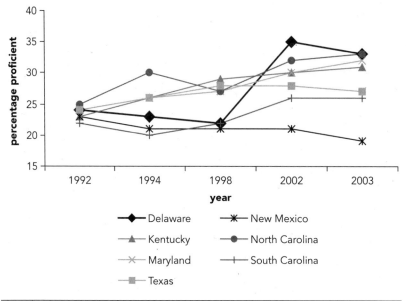

Source: Winograd and Thorstensen 2004.

An analysis of findings can lead to decisions affecting the provision of resources in the education system in general (for example, for the reform of curricula and textbooks or for teacher development) or in categories of schools with particular characteristics (for example, schools in rural areas or schools serving students in socioeconomically disadvantaged areas). Many examples can be found of the use of the findings of national and international assessments for such purposes. They have been used in Australia to provide programs designed to increase the participation and performance of girls in mathematics and science (Keeves 1995); they have prompted curriculum reform in low- and middle-income countries (Elley 2005), have helped divert financial resources to poorer schools in Chile (see A.7 in appendix A), and have promoted teacher professionalism in Uruguay (see A.3 in appendix A).

The results of a national assessment may also be used to change practice in the classroom (Horn, Wolff, and Velez 1992). Getting information to teachers and effecting changes in their behavior that will substantially raise the achievements of students, however, is not an easy task. The pressure on schools and classrooms to change is greatest when the results of a national assessment are based on a census, not a sample, and when high stakes are attached to performance. No specific action may be taken by the authorities apart from the publication of information about performance (for example, in league tables), or sanctions may be attached to performance. Sanctions can take the form of rewards for improved performance (for example, schools, teachers, or both receive economic incentives if students achieve a specific target) or "punishment" for poor performance (for example, nonpromotion of students or dismissal of teachers) (see A.7 in appendix A for a brief description of Chile's reward program).

When a national assessment obtains information about the achievement of students in all (or most) schools, some policy makers may see an opportunity to use these data to judge the quality of teachers and schools. Obviously, teachers and students should bear some responsibility for learning, but the role of institutions, agencies, and individuals that exercise control over the resources and activities of schools should also be reflected in an accountability system. Apportioning fairly the responsibilities of all stakeholders is important, whether an assessment is sample-based or census-based. The national assessment in Uruguay provides a good example of recognition of the responsibility of a variety of stakeholders (including the state) for student achievement (see A.3 in appendix A).

In some cases, a national assessment may simply have a symbolic role, which is designed to legitimate state action by embracing internationally accepted models of modernity and by imbuing the policymaking process with the guise of scientific rationality (Benveniste 2000, 2002; Kellaghan 2003). When this role motivates a national assessment, the act of assessment has greater significance than its outcomes. If a national assessment is carried out simply to meet the requirement of a donor agency, or even to meet a government's international commitments to monitor progress toward achieving the Millennium Development Goals, it may have little more than symbolic value, and its findings may not be seriously considered in the management of the education system or in policy making.

DECISIONS IN A NATIONAL ASSESSMENT

In this chapter, we consider 12 decisions that are involved in planning a national assessment (see Greaney and Kellaghan 1996; Kellaghan 1997; and Kellaghan and Greaney 2001b, 2004).

WHO SHOULD GIVE POLICY GUIDANCE FOR THE NATIONAL ASSESSMENT?

The ministry of education should appoint a national steering committee (NSC) to provide overall guidance to the agency that will carry out the assessment. The committee can help ensure that the national assessment has status and that key policy questions of interest to the ministry and others are addressed. It could also help resolve serious administrative and financial problems that might arise during the implementation of the national assessment. Giving the NSC a degree of ownership over the direction and intent of the national assessment also increases the likelihood that the results of the assessment will play a role in future policy making.

The composition of an NSC will vary from country to country, depending on the power structure within the education system. In addition to representatives of the ministry of education, NSCs might include representatives of major ethnic, religious, and linguistic groups, as well as those groups whose members will be expected to act on the results (such as teacher trainers, teachers, school inspectors, and curriculum personnel). Box 4.1 lists suggested members of a steering committee for a national assessment in Sierra Leone proposed by participants at an international workshop. Addressing the information needs of those various stakeholders should help ensure that the national assessment exercise does not result in a report that is criticized or ignored because of its failure to address the "correct" questions.

The NSC should not be overburdened with meetings and should not be required to address routine implementation tasks related to the national assessment. In some cases, the NSC may provide direction at the initial stage by identifying the purpose of and rationale for the assessment, by determining the curriculum areas and grade levels to be assessed, or by selecting the agency or agencies to conduct the assessment, although those items may also be decided before the committee is established. The NSC is likely to be most active at the

---

BOX 4.1

Proposed NSC Membership in Sierra Leone

- Basic Education Commission
- Civil Society Movement
- Decentralized Secretariat
- Director-General of Education (chair)
- Education Planning Directorate
- Inter-Religious Council
- National Curriculum Research Development Centre
- Sierra Leone Teachers Union
- Statistics Sierra Leone
- Teacher Training Colleges
- West African Examinations Council

start of the assessment exercise, whereas the implementing agency will be responsible for most of the detailed work, such as instrument development, sampling, analysis, and reporting. The implementing agency, however, should provide the NSC with draft copies of tests and questionnaires and with descriptions of proposed procedures so that committee members can provide guidance and can ensure that the information needs that prompted the assessment in the first place are being adequately addressed. NSC members should also review draft reports prepared by the implementing agency.

Responsibility for providing policy guidance: Ministry of education

WHO SHOULD CARRY OUT THE NATIONAL ASSESSMENT?

A national assessment should be carried out by a credible team or organization whose work can command respect and enhance the likelihood of broad-scale acceptance of the findings. Various countries have assigned responsibility for national assessments to groups ranging from teams set up within the ministry of education, to autonomous bodies (universities, research centers), to nonnational technical teams. We would expect a variety of factors to influence such a decision, including levels of national technical capacity, as well as administrative and political circumstances. Table 4.1 lists some potential advantages and disadvantages of different categories of implementation agencies that merit consideration in deciding who should carry out an assessment.

In some cases, traditions and legislation may impose restrictions on the freedom of a ministry of education in choosing an implementing agency. In Argentina, for example, provinces must authorize the curricular contents to be evaluated in the national assessment. Initially, provinces were asked to produce test items; however, many provinces lacked the technical capacity to do so. At a later stage, provinces were presented with a set of sample questions for their endorsement and the Dirección Nacional de Información y Evaluación de la Calidad Educativa (DiNIECE) constructed the final assessment instruments from the pool of preapproved test items. More recently, test items have been designed independently by university personnel and approved by the national Federal Council. The DiNIECE remains

TABLE 4.1

Options for Implementing a National Assessment

Designated agency	Advantages	Disadvantages
Drawn from staff of ministry of education	Likely to be trusted by ministry. Enjoys ready access to key personnel, materials, and data (for example, school population data). Funds that may not have to be secured for staff time.	Findings might be subject to political manipulation including suppression. May be viewed skeptically by other stakeholders. Staff who may be required to undertake many other tasks. Technical capacity who may be lacking.
Drawn from staff of public examination unit	Usually is credible. Has experience in running secure assessments. Funds that may not have to be secured for staff time. Some skills (for example, test development) that can be transferred to enhance the examination unit. More likely to be sustainable than some other models.	Staff who may be required to undertake many other tasks. Technical capacity that may be weak. May lack ready access to data. Public examination experience that may result in test items that are too difficult.
Drawn from research/ university sector	Findings that may be more credible with stakeholders. Greater likelihood of some technical competence. May use data for further studies of the education system.	Have to raise funds to cover staff costs. May be less sustainable than some other models. May come into conflict with education ministry.

Designated agency	Advantages	Disadvantages
Recruited as foreign technical assistance (TA)	More likely to be technically competent. Nature of funding that can help ensure timely completion.	Likely to be expensive. May not be sensitive to educational context. Difficult to ensure assessment sustainability. Possibly little national capacity enhancement.
Made up of a national team supported with some international TA	Can improve technical capacity of nationals. May ensure timely completion. May add credibility to the results.	Possibly difficult to coordinate work of national team members and TA. Might be difficult to ensure skill transfer to nationals.
Ministry team supported with national TA	Can ensure ministry support while obtaining national TA. Less expensive than international TA.	National TA that may lack the necessary technical capacity. Other potential disadvantages that are listed under ministry of education and that may apply.

Source: Authors.

responsible for the design of achievement tests, the analyses of results, and the general coordination of annual assessment activities.

It is worth reflecting on the wide variety of skills that are required to carry out a national assessment in deciding who should be given responsibility for the task. This issue is addressed in more detail in *Implementing a National Assessment of Educational Achievement* (book 3 in this series). A national assessment is fundamentally a team effort. The team should be flexible, willing to work under pressure and in a collaborative manner, and prepared to learn new assessment and technological approaches. The team leader should have strong managerial skills. He or she will be required to organize the staff, to coordinate and schedule activities, to support training, and to arrange and monitor finance. The team leader should be politically astute because he or she will need to report to an NSC and to be a liaison with national, regional, and, in some instances, district-level government bodies and representatives of stakeholders (such as teachers and religious bodies).

The team should have high-level implementation or operational skills. Tasks to be completed include organizing workshops for item writers and test administrators; arranging for printing and distribution of tests, questionnaires, and manuals; contacting schools; developing training materials; and collecting and recording data. A small dedicated team of test developers will be needed to analyze the curriculum, develop tables of specifications or a test blueprint, draft items, select items after pretesting or piloting, and advise on scoring. Following test administration, open-ended and multiple-choice questions have to be scored.

The team will require support from one or more people with statistical and analytical competence in selecting samples, in weighting data, in data input and file preparation, in item analysis of test data as well as general statistical analysis of the overall results, and in preparing data files for others (for example, academics and postgraduate students) to carry out secondary analyses. Many developing countries lack capacity in this last area, leading to situations in which data are collected but never adequately analyzed or reported.

The team should have the necessary personnel to draft and disseminate results, press releases, and focused pamphlets or newsletters.

It might also be reasonably expected to play a key role in organizing workshops for teachers and other education officials so they can discuss the importance of the results and the results' implications for teaching and learning.

Most members of the team may work part time and be employed as needed. This category could include item writers—especially practicing teachers with a good knowledge of the curriculum—and experts in sampling and statistical analysis. Team members might be recruited from outside the education sector. For example, a national census bureau can be a good source of sampling expertise. Computer personnel with relevant experience could help with data cleaning, and journalists could assist with drafting catchy press releases. Neither Cambodia nor Ethiopia employed full-time staff members to carry out its national assessment.

Responsibility for carrying out national assessment: Implementation agency (ministry of education, examination board, research agency, university).

WHO WILL ADMINISTER THE TESTS AND QUESTIONNAIRES?

National administrative traditions and perceptions of levels of trust, as well as sources of finance, tend to influence the selection of personnel responsible for administering tests and questionnaires in a national assessment. Practice varies. For example, some countries have used graduate students, while Zambia has involved school inspectors and ministry officials in test and questionnaire administration. Other countries have used experienced teachers drawn from nonparticipating schools or retired teachers. In the Maldives, a test administrator must be a staff member of a school located on an island other than the island where the targeted school is located.

Test administrators should be carefully selected. They should have good organizational skills, have experience of working in schools, and be committed to following test and questionnaire guidelines precisely. Ideally, they should have classroom experience, speak in the same language and accent as the students, and have an authoritative but nonthreatening manner. Book 3 of this series, *Implementing a National*

Assessment of Educational Achievement, considers the advantages and disadvantages of having teachers, inspectors, teacher trainers, examination board personnel, and university students as administrators.

Although the use of teachers of students who are participating in the national assessment as test administrators may appear administratively convenient and very cost-effective, it is, for a variety of reasons, rarely done. Some teachers might feel that their teaching effectiveness is being evaluated. Some may find it difficult to desist from their normal practice of trying to help students and might not be able to adjust to the formal testing approach. Some may make copies of tests or test items, thus ruling out the possibility of using those items in future national assessments. Having teachers administer tests to their own students might also diminish the public perception of the trustworthiness of the assessment results.

Responsibility for administering tests and questionnaires: Implementation agency

WHAT POPULATION WILL BE ASSESSED?

As the term is usually understood, national assessments refer to surveys carried out in education systems. This connotation, however, was not always the case. When the first national assessment was carried out in the United States (in 1969), out-of-school populations (17- and 18-year-olds and young adults 26–35 years of age), as well as school-going populations, were assessed (in citizenship, reading, and science). The assessment of the out-of-school populations was discontinued, however, because of cost (Jones 2003). Subsequent surveys of adult literacy were carried out independent of national assessments.

The issue of assessing younger out-of-school children is more relevant in many developing countries than in the United States because many children of school-going age do not attend school. Obviously, the achievements (or lack of them) of those children are of interest to policy makers and politicians and may have particular relevance for the nonformal education sector. Their inclusion in a conventional national assessment is, however, difficult to envisage. Although particular groups of out-of-school youth might be assessed using national assessment tests in a separate study, methods of assessment and sampling procedures generally would be very different, and the varying circumstances of such children (for example, special needs, socioeconomic disadvantage, or distance from school) would have to be taken into account.

As far as school-going children are concerned, policy makers want information about their knowledge and skills at selected points in their educational careers. A decision has to be made about whether populations are defined on the basis of age or grade or, indeed, by a combination of age and grade. In countries where students vary widely in the age at which they enter school, and in which policies of non-promotion are in operation, students of similar age will not be concentrated in the same grade. In this situation, a strong argument can be made for targeting grade level rather than age.

The grade to be assessed should normally be dictated by the information needs of the ministry of education. If, for example, the ministry is interested in finding out about the learning achievement levels of students completing primary school, it might request that a national assessment be carried out toward the end of the last year of primary school (fifth or sixth grade in many countries). The ministry could also request a national assessment in third or fourth grade if it needed data on how students are performing midway through the basic education cycle. This information could then be used to introduce remedial measures (such as in-service courses for teachers) to address problems with specific aspects of the curriculum identified in the assessment.

Target grades for national assessments have varied from country to country. In the United States, student achievement levels are assessed at grades 4, 8, and 12; in Colombia, achievement is assessed at grades 3, 5, 7, and 9; in Uruguay, at preschool and at grades 1, 2, and 6; and in Sri Lanka, at grades 4, 8, and 10. In anglophone Africa, a regional consortium of education systems, the Southern and Eastern Africa Consortium for Monitoring Educational Quality (SACMEQ), assessed grade 6 students. Countries in the francophone African consortium Programme d'Analyse des Systèmes Educatifs de la CONFEMEN (Conférence des Ministres de l'Education des Pays ayant le Français en Partage) assessed students in grades 2 and 5.

Sometimes pragmatic considerations dictate grade selection. The Nigerian Federal Ministry of Education decided to assess students in grade 4 because testing at any lower level would have required translation of tests into many local languages. More senior grades were not considered suitable because students and teachers would be focused on secondary-school entrance examinations.

Relatively few countries conduct large-scale assessments in grades 1 to 3. Students at that level might not be able to follow instructions or to cope with the cognitive tasks of the assessment or with the challenge of completing multiple-choice tests. A Jamaican study noted that a sizable number of grade 1 students were unable to recognize the letters of the alphabet (Lockheed and Harris 2005). Nevertheless, we should bear in mind that because information about early student learning patterns may be critical to reform efforts, alternative procedures to monitor those patterns should be in place.

Responsibility for selecting population to be assessed: Ministry of education and NSC

WILL A WHOLE POPULATION OR A SAMPLE BE ASSESSED?

Most national and all regional and international studies use sample-based approaches in determining national achievement levels. Some national assessments have used both census- and sample-based approaches (for example, Costa Rica, Cuba, France, Honduras, Jordan, Mexico, and Uruguay), whereas most subnational assessments collect census data (for example, Minas Gerais, Parana, and São Paulo, Brazil; Bogotá, Colombia; and Aguascalientes, Mexico) (see Crespo, Soares, and deMello e Souza 2000). Several factors favor the use of a sample if the objective is to obtain information for policy purposes on the functioning of the education system as a whole. Those factors include (a) reduced costs in test administration and in cleaning and managing data, (b) less time required for analysis and reporting, and (c) greater accuracy because of the possibility of providing more intense supervision of fieldwork and data preparation (Ross 1987).

As noted in chapter 3, the purpose of an assessment is key in determining whether to test a sample or the entire population of targeted

TABLE 4.2

Advantages and Disadvantages of Census-Based Assessment to Hold Schools Accountable

Advantages	Disadvantages
Focuses on what are considered important aspects of education.	Tends to lead to neglect of subject areas that are not tested.
Highlights important aspects of individual subjects.	Tends to lead to neglect of aspects of subjects that are not tested (such as oral fluency in language).
Helps ensure that students reach an acceptable standard before promotion.	Has contributed to early dropout and nonpromotion.
Allows for direct comparisons of schools.	Leads to unfair ranking of schools where different social backgrounds are served and where results are not significantly different.
Builds public confidence in the performance of the system.	Has led to cheating during test administration and to subsequent doctoring of results.
Puts pressure on students to learn.	Tends to emphasize memorization and rote learning.
Results in some schools and students raising test performance levels.	Improved performance may be limited to a particular test and will not be evident on other tests of the same subject area.
Allows parents to judge the effectiveness of individual schools and teachers.	Leads to unfair assessment of effectiveness on the basis of test score performance rather than taking into account other established factors related to learning achievement.
Tends to be popular with politicians and media.	Seldom holds politicians accountable for failure to support delivery of educational resources.

Source: Authors.

students. On the one hand, the decision to involve an entire population may reflect an intention to foster school, teacher, or even student accountability. It facilitates the use of sanctions (incentives or penalties), the provision of feedback to individual schools on performance, and the publication of league tables, as well as the identification of schools with the greatest need for assistance (for example, as in Chile and Mexico). On the other hand, the sample-based approach will permit the detection of problems only at the system level. It will not identify specific schools in need of support, although it can identify types or categories of schools (for example, small rural schools) that require attention. It can also identify problems relating to gender or ethnic equity.

An argument against the use of a sample-based approach is that because the assessment does not have high stakes attached to performance, some students will not be motivated to take the test seriously. That was not the case, however, in many countries—including South Africa—where some students were afraid that performance on the Trends in International Mathematics and Science Study (TIMSS) tests would count toward their official school results. It is interesting to note that cheating occurred during test administration, presumably because of the perception that relatively high stakes were attached to performance (see A.4 in appendix A).

Advantages and disadvantages of using a national assessment to hold schools, teachers, and sometimes students accountable are set out in table 4.2. The topics listed are derived for the most part from studies of the effects of high-stakes public examinations, not from a study of national assessments. Nevertheless, they should be relevant to census-based national assessments, at least to ones that act as surrogate public examinations (as in the United States and some Latin American countries).

Responsibility for deciding whether to use a sample or census: Ministry of education

WHAT WILL BE ASSESSED?

All national assessments measure cognitive outcomes of instruction or scholastic skills in the areas of language/literacy and mathematics/numeracy, a reflection of the importance of those outcomes for basic education. In some countries, knowledge of science and social studies is included in an assessment. Whatever the domain of the assessment, providing an appropriate framework is important, in the first instance for constructing assessment instruments and afterward for interpreting results. The framework may be available in a curriculum document if, for example, the document provides expectations for learning that are clearly prioritized and put into operation. In most cases, however, such a framework will not be available, and those charged with the national assessment will have to construct it. In that task, close cooperation will be required between the assessment agency, those responsible for curricula, and other stakeholders.

Assessment frameworks attempt to clarify in detail what is being assessed in a large-scale assessment, how it is being assessed, and why it is being assessed (see Kirsch 2001). The aim of the framework is to make the assessment process and the assumptions behind it transparent, not just for test developers but also for a much larger audience, including teachers, curriculum personnel, and policy makers. The framework usually starts with a general definition or statement of purpose that guides the rationale for the assessment and that specifies what should be measured in terms of knowledge, skills, and other attributes. It then identifies and describes various performances or behaviors that will reveal those constructs by identifying a specific number of characteristic tasks or variables to be used in developing the assessment, and it indicates how those performances are to be used to assess student performance (Mullis and others 2006).

Many national assessments have been based on a content analysis at a particular grade level of what students are expected to have learned as a result of exposure to a prescribed or intended curriculum. Typically, this analysis is done in a matrix with cognitive behaviors on the horizontal axis and with themes or content areas on the vertical axis. Thus, the intersection of a cognitive behavior and content area will represent a learning objective. Cells may be weighted in terms of their importance.

Recent national (and international) assessments have drawn on research relating to the development in students of literary and numeracy skills that may or may not be represented in national curricula. For example, in the International Association for the Evaluation of Educational Achievement (IEA) *Framework and Specifications* document for the Progress in International Reading Literacy Study (PIRLS) 2006, reading literacy is defined as "the ability to understand and use those written language forms required by society and/or valued by the individual. Young readers can construct meaning from a variety of texts. They read to learn, to participate in communities of readers in school and everyday life, and for enjoyment" (Mullis and others 2006, 3). From this definition it is evident that reading is much more than decoding text or getting the meaning of a passage or poem. PIRLS further clarified what it proposed to measure by indicating the process and tasks to be assessed and the percentages of test items devoted to each (table 4.3).

The framework document specified that the assessment would use test booklets with five literary and five informational passages and that each passage would be followed by 12 questions, half of which

TABLE 4.3

PIRLS Reading Comprehension Processes

Comprehension processes	Examples of tasks	Items
Focus on and retrieve explicitly stated information	Looking for specific ideas. Finding definitions or phrases Identifying the setting for a story (for example, time, place). Finding topic sentence or main idea (explicitly stated).	20%
Make straightforward inferences	Inferring that one event caused another. Identifying generalizations in text. Describing the relationship between characters. Determining the referent of a pronoun.	30%
Interpret and integrate ideas and information	Determining the overall message or theme. Contrasting text information. Inferring a story's mood or tone. Interpreting a real-world application of text information.	30%
Examine and evaluate content, language, and textual elements	Evaluating the likelihood that the events described could happen. Describing how the author devised a surprise ending. Judging the completeness or clarity of information in text. Determining the author's perspectives.	20%

Source: Campbell and others 2001; Mullis and others 2006.

would be multiple choice and half would be constructed response. It also indicated that because reading attitudes and behaviors were important for the development of a lifelong reading habit and were related to reading achievement, PIRLS would include items in the student questionnaire to assess student reading attitudes and behaviors. It justified its selection of students in the fourth year of formal schooling as the target population for the assessment on the basis that the fourth year represented the transition stage from learning to read to reading to learn.

In its assessment framework, PIRLS recognized two main purposes that students have for reading:

- Reading for literacy experience
- Reading to acquire and use information.

It also gave a detailed justification for the emphasis that PIRLS placed on finding out more about the environment and the context in which students learn to read. This emphasis led to the inclusion of questionnaire items on home characteristics that can encourage children to learn to read: literacy-related activities of parents, language spoken in the home, links between the home and the school, and students' out-of-school literacy activities. School-level items covered school resources that can directly or indirectly affect reading achievement. The framework document also justified assessing classroom variables, such as instructional approaches and the nature of teacher training.

A further alternative to basing an assessment instrument on curriculum-embedded expectations or prescriptions, which is feasible in the case of older students, is to build a test to reflect the knowledge and skills that students are likely to need and build on in adult life. The Programme for International Student Assessment (PISA) provided an example of this method when it set out to assess the "mathematical literacy" of 15-year-olds, defined as the "capacity to identify and understand the role that mathematics plays in the world, to make well-founded judgements and to use and engage with mathematics in works that meet the needs of the individual's life as a constructive, concerned, and reflective citizen" (OECD 2003, 24) (see B.3 in appendix B). Although this approach fitted well in an international study, given that the alternative of devising an assessment instrument that would be equally appropriate to a variety of curricula is obviously problematic, it might also be used in a national assessment.

A few national assessments have collected information on affective outcomes (for example, student attitudes to school and student self-esteem). In Colombia, for example, students' attitudes to peace are assessed. Although those outcomes are very important, their measurement tends to be less reliable than the measurement of cognitive outcomes, and analyses based on them have proved difficult to interpret. In Chile, technical difficulties in measuring student values and attitudes to learning led to abandoning those areas (see A.7 in appendix A).

One large-scale assessment (Monitoring Learning Achievement) assessed "life skills," defined as students' knowledge of, and attitudes toward, health and nutrition, environment, civic responsibility, and science and technology (Chinapah 1997). While it is generally accepted that life skills are important and should be taught, there is considerable disagreement about their precise nature. Their measurement has also proven difficult.

Most national assessments collect information on student, school, and home factors that are considered relevant to student achievement (for example, student gender and educational history, including grade repetition; resources in schools, including the availability of textbooks; level of teacher education and qualifications; and socioeconomic status of students' families). The information is normally collected in questionnaires (and sometimes in interviews) administered to students, to teachers, to principal teachers, and sometimes to parents at the same time as the assessment instruments are administered.

Identification of contextual factors related to student achievement can help identify manipulable variables, that is, factors that can be altered by policy makers, such as regulations about the time allocated to curriculum areas, textbook provision, and class size. The contextual data collected in some national (and international) studies, however, cannot play this role because they do not adequately measure the conditions in which students live. Economic status, for example, may be based on a list of items that includes a car, a television set, and a water tap in a country where the majority of the population lives at least part of the year on less than the equivalent of US$1 a day. Furthermore, despite the relevance of health status and nutritional status, no information may be obtained about them (Naumann 2005).

In some assessments, teachers' (as well as pupils') achievements have been assessed. In Vietnam (see A.2 in appendix A) and a number of African countries in the SACMEQ studies (see C.1 in appendix C), teachers were required to take the same test items as their students to gain some insight into teachers' levels of subject mastery. In Uganda, information was obtained on the extent to which teachers claimed to be familiar with key official curriculum documents.

Responsibility for deciding what will be assessed: Ministry of education, NSC, with input from implementation agency.

HOW WILL ACHIEVEMENT BE ASSESSED?

An instrument or instruments must be devised that will provide the information that the national assessment is meant to obtain. Because the purposes and proposed uses of national assessments vary, so too will the instruments used in the assessments and the ways results are reported.

Some national assessments present results in terms of the characteristics of the distribution of test scores—for example, the mean percentage of items that students answered correctly and the way scores were distributed around the mean. Or results might be scaled to an arbitrary mean (such as 500) and standard deviation (such as 100). Although these scores can be used to compare the performance of subgroups in the sample, they are limited in their use in a national assessment, primarily because they tell us little about students' level of subject matter knowledge or the actual skills that students have acquired.

To address this issue, and to make the results of an assessment more meaningful for stakeholders, an increasing number of national assessments seek to report results in a way that specifies what students know and do not know and that identifies strengths and weaknesses in their knowledge and skills. This approach involves matching student scores with descriptions of the tasks they are able to do (for example, "can read at a specified level of comprehension" or "can carry out basic mathematical operations"). Performances may be categorized in various ways (for example, "satisfactory" or "unsatisfactory"; "basic," "proficient," or "advanced"), and the proportion of students achieving at each level determined. Matching student scores to performance levels is a complex task involving the judgment of curriculum experts and statistical analysts.

The way in which results will be described should be a consideration at the test development stage. Thus, test development might begin with specification of a framework in which expectations for learning are posited, following which test items are written to assess the extent to which students meet those expectations. If items do not meet certain criteria when tried out, however, including the extent to which they discriminate between students, they may not be included in the final assessment instrument. Care should be taken to ensure that important curriculum objectives are reflected in an assessment, even if no students in the trial provide evidence of achieving them.

Most national and international assessments rely to a considerable extent on the multiple-choice format in their instruments. Those items will often be supplemented by open-ended items that require the student to write a word, phrase, or sentence. Examples of multiple-choice and open-ended items are provided in box 4.2 and box 4.3, respectively.

In several national (for example, the U.S. NAEP and Ireland's National Assessment of English Reading) and international assessments (for example, TIMSS and PISA), each student responds to only a fraction of the total number of items used in an assessment (see A.8 in appendix A; B.1 and B.3 in appendix B). This approach increases overall test coverage of the curriculum without placing too great a burden on individual students. It also allows the use of extended passages (for example, a short story or a newspaper article) in the assessment of reading comprehension. In other assessments, all students respond to the same set of items. Although some advantages are associated with having individual students respond to only a fraction of items, disadvantages also exist, particularly for countries beginning a national assessment program. Administration (for example, printing and distribution) is more complex, as is scoring and scaling of

BOX 4.2

Examples of Multiple-Choice Items

Subject: Geography

The river Volga is in

A. China

B. Germany

C. Russia

D. Sweden.

Subject: Mathematics

A seal has to breathe if it is asleep. Martin observed a seal for one hour. At the start of this observation, the seal dived to the bottom of the sea and started to sleep. In eight minutes, it slowly floated to the surface and took a breath. In three minutes, it was back at the bottom of the sea again, and the whole process started over in a very regular way. After one hour, the seal was

A. at the bottom

B. on its way up

C. breathing

D. on its way down.

Source: Mathematics example: OECD 2007. Reproduced with permission.

BOX 4.3

Examples of Open-Ended Items

Subject: Language

TALL is the opposite of SMALL.

What is the opposite of

QUICK _____   DARK _____

HEAVY _____   OLD _____

Subject: Mathematics

Use your ruler to draw a rectangle with a perimeter of 20 centimeters. Label the width and the length.

scores, while analyses involving individual student or school data can be problematic (see Sofroniou and Kellaghan 2004).

The issue of language of assessment is generally accorded less attention than it deserves. It is associated with two problems. First, although in many countries large minority (and sometimes majority) groups are present for whom the language of instruction is not their mother tongue, students are usually assessed in the language of instruction. In Uganda, for example, the vast majority of students take tests in their second language (see A.9 in appendix A). Poor performance on tests is attributed to this practice, as are the generally poor scholastic progress of students and early dropout rates from school (Naumann 2005).

A second problem relating to language arises if the instruments of the assessment need to be translated into one or more languages. If comparisons are to be made between performances assessed in different languages, analysis must take into account the possibility that differences that may emerge may be attributable to language-related differences in the difficulty of assessment tasks. The issue is partly addressed by changing words. For example, in an international assessment carried out in South Africa, words such as "gasoline" ("petrol") and "flashlight" ("torch") were changed. Ghana replaced the word "snow" with "rain." If language differences co-vary with cultural and economic factors, the problem is compounded because it may be difficult to ensure the equivalence of the way questions are phrased and the cultural appropriateness of content in all language versions of a test. For example, material that is context-appropriate for students in rural areas—covering hunting, the local marketplace, agricultural pursuits, and local games—might be unfamiliar to students in urban areas.

Whatever the details of the method of assessment, the assessment needs to provide valid and reliable information. Validity has several facets, including the adequacy of an assessment instrument to sample and represent the construct (for example, reading literacy) or the curriculum area (for example, social studies) identified in the assessment framework. The judgment of curriculum specialists is important here. Furthermore, the assessment instrument should measure only what it is designed to measure. For example, a test of mathematics or science should assess students' knowledge and skills in those areas, not their competence in language. The reliability of assessment procedures in national assessments usually involves estimating the extent to which individual items in a test assess the overall construct the test is designed to measure and, in the case of open-ended items, the extent to which two or more markers agree in their scoring.

Responsibility for deciding how achievement will be assessed: Implementation agency.

HOW FREQUENTLY WILL ASSESSMENTS BE CARRIED OUT?

The frequency with which a national assessment is carried out varies from country to country, ranging from every year to every 10 years. A temptation may exist to assess achievement in the same curriculum areas and in the same population every year, but this frequency is unnecessary, as well as very expensive, if the aim is to monitor national standards. In the United States, reading and mathematics are assessed every second year and other subjects less frequently. The international assessment of reading literacy (PIRLS) had a five-year span between the first and second administration (2001–06). In Japan, achievement in core curriculum areas was assessed every 10 years to guide curriculum and textbook revision (Ishino 1995).

If the aim of an assessment is to hold teachers, schools, and even students accountable for their learning, testing may be carried out every year. Furthermore, because such an assessment focuses on the performance of individuals, as well as performance at the system level, all (or most) students in the education system will be assessed. This system has been operated in Chile and in England.

If the purpose of an assessment is only to provide information on the performance of the system as a whole, however, an assessment of a sample of students in a particular curriculum area every three to five years would seem adequate. Because education systems do not change rapidly, more frequent assessments would be unlikely to register change. Overfrequent assessments would more than likely limit the impact of the results, as well as incur unnecessary costs.

Responsibility for deciding frequency of assessment: Ministry of education

HOW SHOULD STUDENT ACHIEVEMENT BE REPORTED?

Although policy makers probably prefer summary statistics, evidence on the multidimensionality of achievement suggests that a single index of performance, such as a total test score, may obscure important information. An alternative approach is to provide differentiated information that reflects strengths and weaknesses in a country's curriculum. The information would be even more valuable if it distinguished between students' knowledge of basic facts and skills and their deeper or higher-order understanding.

A variety of procedures have been used to describe student achievements in national assessments, which reflect the richness of the data that an assessment can provide (see book 5 in this series, *Reporting and Using Results from a National Assessment of Educational Achievement*). The selection of one or more procedures should be guided by the information needs of the ministry of education and other stakeholders.

Item-Level Information

This information involves little more than simply reporting the percentage of students answering individual items correctly. A national assessment might reveal that the majority of its students performed poorly on a mathematics item involving the use of indices, or that virtually all students were able to associate simple words with pictures. In Ghana, for example, only 1 percent of students correctly answered a question on light refraction in TIMSS (Ghana, Ministry of Education, Youth, and Sports 2004). This kind of information, while too detailed for national policy making, is likely to be of interest to curriculum personnel, teacher trainers, and possibly textbook authors.

Performance in Curriculum Domains

Items can be grouped into curriculum units or domains, and test scores can be reported in terms of performance in each domain. Reading items, for example, have been classified by ability to retrieve information from a text, to make inferences from a text, to interpret

FIGURE 4.1

Mean Percentage Correct Scores for Students' Mathematics Performance, by Content Area, Lesotho

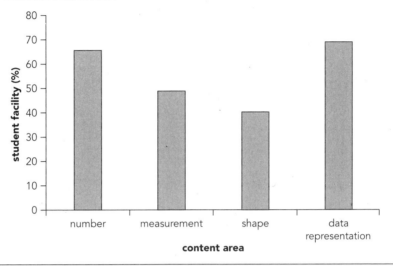

Source: Lesotho, Examinations Council of Lesotho and National Curriculum Development Centre 2006.

and integrate information, and to examine and evaluate text information (Eivers and others 2005). Figure 4.1 illustrates how Lesotho reported mathematics performance by content area.

Performance Standards

Performance on national and international assessments describes how well students perform on the test to achieve a "basic," "proficient," or "advanced" level in a curriculum area. The number of levels may vary (see A.2 in appendix A for a description of six levels of reading proficiency used in a national assessment in Vietnam, and see C.1 in appendix C for eight reading levels and eight mathematics skill levels used in SACMEQ). The selection of cutoff points between levels involves the use of statistical data and subjective judgment.

Mastery Standard

Mastery levels can be based on an overall test score (for example, correctly answering a specified percentage of test items). In Sri Lanka, the mastery level for a grade 4 national assessment was set at 80 percent. Fewer than 40 percent achieved that level in the students' first language or in mathematics, and fewer than 10 percent in English (Perera and others 2004). Mastery levels can also be based on achieving a certain performance level. In the United States, five levels of performance ("below basic," "basic," "proficient," "goal," and "advanced") are used in Connecticut. The "goal" level is regarded as a challenging but reasonable level of expectation for students and is accepted as the mastery level. The data in table 4.4 show that well over half the students in grades 3 and 4 achieved the "goal" or "mastery" level in all three curriculum areas.

Responsibility for deciding how student achievement is reported: Implementation agency with input from NSC

WHAT KINDS OF STATISTICAL ANALYSES SHOULD BE CARRIED OUT?

Some analyses will be dictated by the policy questions that prompted the assessment in the first instance. Most national assessments provide evidence on achievement by gender, region, urban or rural location, ethnic or language group membership, and type of institution attended (public or private). Some assessments also provide data on the quality of school facilities (for example, Kenya). Analyses involving those variables are relatively straightforward and are intuitively meaningful to policy makers and politicians. They do not, however, adequately represent the complexity of the data. More complex forms of analysis are required if we are, for example, to throw light on the school and background factors that contribute to achievement. Examples of the use of complex statistical procedures are found in the description of the Vietnamese national assessment (see A.2 in appendix A).

The limitations of analyses and problems in inferring causation from studies in which data are collected at the same time on achievement and other variables should be recognized. Although it is difficult, sometimes impossible, to disentangle the effects of community, home, and school factors on students' learning, this complexity has not deterred

TABLE 4.4

Percentage Achieving Goal or Mastery Level by Grade, Connecticut, 2006

Grade	Mathematics		Reading		Writing	
	At or above goal (%)	At or above advanced (%)	At or above goal (%)	At or above advanced (%)	At or above goal (%)	At or above advanced (%)
3	56	22	54	17	61	22
4	59	22	58	16	63	22

Source: Connecticut Department of Education 2006.

some investigations from causally interpreting data collected in national and international assessments.

Responsibility for deciding on methods of statistical analysis: Implementation agency.

HOW SHOULD THE RESULTS OF A NATIONAL ASSESSMENT BE COMMUNICATED AND USED?

If the results of a national assessment are to affect national education policy, they should be reported as soon as possible after the completion of data analysis. In the past, technical reports that featured a considerable amount of data tended to be the sole form of reporting. Some groups of users (for example, teachers in Chile; see A.7 in appendix A), however, considered those reports overtechnical. As a result, the requirement to provide other forms of reports is now increasingly recognized. Those alternatives include short summary reports that focus on the main findings for busy policy makers; press releases; special reports for radio and television; and separate reports for schools, teachers, curriculum developers, and teacher trainers. In some countries (for example, Sri Lanka), separate reports are prepared for each province. A report in Ethiopia was translated into four major languages. The information needs of stakeholders should determine the contents of additional reports.

The ministry of education should make adequate budgetary provision at the planning stage for report preparation and dissemination. In collaboration with the national steering committee, it should devise procedures to communicate the findings of national assessments to stakeholders. Appropriate strategies to communicate results should take into account the fact that users (whether administrators or teachers) vary greatly in their ability to understand and apply statistical information in their decision making. Obviously, there is no point in producing reports if the information they contain is not adequately disseminated. Thus, a dissemination strategy is also required so that relevant information reaches all stakeholders. The strategy should identify potential users (key institutions and individuals) and their levels of technical expertise.

National assessment results have been used to set benchmarks for monitoring learning achievement levels (for example, in Lesotho), reforming curricula, providing baseline data on the amount and quality of educational materials in schools (for example, in Vietnam), identifying correlates of achievement, and diagnosing aspects of the curriculum that are not being mastered by students. Uruguay, for instance, used its national assessment results to help prepare teacher guides and to identify the curriculum content and behavioral areas that subsequently helped direct a large-scale teacher in-service program (see A.3 in appendix A).

Book 5 in this series, *Reporting and Using Results from a National Assessment of Educational Achievement*, has an extensive section on report writing and the use of national assessment results.

Responsibility for communicating and using national assessment results: Implementation agency, ministry of education, NSC, teacher training providers, curriculum authority, teachers.

WHAT ARE THE COST COMPONENTS OF A NATIONAL ASSESSMENT?

The cost of a national assessment will vary greatly from one country to another, depending on the salary levels of personnel and the cost of services. Within a country, cost will also vary, depending on some or all of the following factors (Ilon 1996).

- *Implementing agency.* Costs will vary depending on whether the agency has the necessary facilities and expertise or needs to upgrade or employ full-time or part-time consultants. The cost of providing facilities and equipment, including computers and software, also needs to be taken into account.

- *Instrument content and construction.* Options for the selection of the content and form of assessment should be considered in terms of cost, as well as other factors, such as validity and ease of administration. Multiple-choice items are more expensive to construct than open-ended items but are usually less expensive to score. The cost of translating tests, questionnaires, and manuals and of training item writers also needs to be considered.

- *Numbers of participating schools and students.* A census-based assessment will obviously be more expensive than a sample-based one. Costs increase if reliable data are required for sectors of the system (for example, states or provinces). Targeting an age level is likely to be more expensive than targeting a grade level because students of any particular age may be spread over a number of grades, requiring additional assessment material and testing sessions.

- *Administration.* Data collection tends to be the most expensive component of a national assessment. It involves obtaining information from schools in advance of the assessment; designing, printing, packaging, and dispatching test materials and questionnaires; and establishing a system to administer instruments. Factors that contribute to overall cost include (a) the number of schools and students that participate, (b) travel, (c) difficulty in gaining access to schools, (d) accommodation for enumerators (if needed), and (e) the collection and return of completed tests and questionnaires.

- *Scoring, data management, and data entry.* Costs will vary according to the number of participating schools, students, teachers, and parents; the number of open-ended items; whether items are hand or machine scored; the number of inter-rater reliability studies; and the quality of test administration and scoring.

- *Analysis.* Analytic costs will depend on the type of assessment procedures used and the availability of technology for scoring and analysis. Although machine scoring is normally considered to be cheaper than hand scoring, this reduced cost may not be the case in a country where technology costs are high and labor costs are low.

- *Reporting.* Costing should take account of the fact that different versions of a report will be required for policy makers, teachers, and the general public and of the nature and extent of the report dissemination strategy.

- *Follow-up activities.* Budgetary provision may have to be made for activities such as in-service teacher training that is based on the findings of the national assessment, briefings for curriculum bodies, and secondary analyses of the data. Provision may also have to be made to address skill shortages in key professional areas (for example, statistical analysis). Budgetary provision should be made for likely salary increases over the life of the assessment (normally two to three years), for inflation, and for unexpected events (contingencies).

Some national assessments have not achieved their basic objectives because the budget was inadequate. Although the overall budget is the responsibility of the ministry of education, people with expertise in costing and with large-scale data projects should participate in the budgetary discussions. Ministry officials who are unfamiliar with large-scale data projects are unlikely to appreciate the need to budget for activities such as pilot-testing and data cleaning.

Figures for the U.S. NAEP provide a rough guide to costing: data collection (30 percent), instrument development (15 percent), data analysis (15 percent), reporting and dissemination (15 percent), sampling (10 percent), data processing (10 percent), and governance (5 percent) (Ilon 1996). In some countries, where, for example, ministry or examination board officials carry out test administration as part of their normal duties, separate budgetary provision may not be made for some activities. Costs and wages will vary depending on national economic conditions. In Cambodia (which is ranked outside the top 100 countries in the world in terms of gross national income), item writers were paid the equivalent of US$5 a day in 2006.

Countries with very limited resources may not find expending those resources on a national assessment advisable, especially when their education system is likely to have many unmet needs. If they do wish to engage in national assessment activity, they would be well advised to limit the number of curriculum areas assessed (perhaps to one, at one grade level) and to seek technical assistance and the support of donors.

In considering costs, it is well to bear in mind that the cost of accountability programs in general—and of national assessments in particular—is very small compared to the cost of other educational programs (see Hoxby 2002). The cost of *not* carrying out an assessment—of not finding out what is working and what is not working in the education system—is likely to be much greater than the cost of an assessment. Book 3 of this series, *Implementing a National Assessment of Educational Achievement*, discusses issues relating to costing a national assessment.

Responsibility for estimating the component costs of a national assessment: Ministry of education with consultant input.

SUMMARY OF DECISIONS

Table 4.5 identifies the agencies with primary responsibility for decisions relating to the 12 components of a national assessment that are discussed in this chapter.

TABLE 4.5

Bodies with Primary Responsibility for Decisions in a National Assessment

Decision	Primary responsibility			
	Ministry of education	National Steering Committee	Agency	Other
Give policy guidance	•			
Carry out national assessment			•	
Administer tests and questionnaires			•	
Choose population to be assessed	•	•		
Determine sample or population	•			
Decide what to assess	•	•	•	
Decide how achievement is assessed			•	
Determine frequency of assessment	•			
Select methods of reporting		•	•	
Determine statistical procedures			•	
Identify methods of communicating and using results	•	•	•	•
Estimate cost components	•			•

Source: Authors.

CHAPTER 5

ISSUES IN THE DESIGN, IMPLEMENTATION, ANALYSIS, REPORTING, AND USE OF A NATIONAL ASSESSMENT

In this chapter, we identify a number of issues that are relevant to the confidence that stakeholders can have in the results of a national assessment. For five components of national assessment activity (design, implementation, data analysis, report writing, and dissemination and use of findings), we suggest a number of activities that will enhance confidence, which, in turn, should contribute to the optimum use of findings. For each component, we also identify common errors that have been made in national assessments and that evaluators should be aware of and should avoid.

DESIGN

The design of the assessment sets out the broad parameters of the exercise: the achievements to be assessed, the grade or age level at which students will be assessed, the policy issues to be addressed, and whether the assessment will involve the whole population or a sample of students.

Recommended Activities

- Involve senior policy makers from the outset to ensure political support and to help frame the assessment design.
- Determine and address the information needs of policy makers when selecting aspects of the curriculum, grade levels, and population subgroups (for example, by region or by gender) to be assessed.
- Obtain teacher support by involving teacher representatives in assessment-related policy decisions.
- Be aware that attaching high stakes to students' performance may lead to teacher opposition and to a narrowing of the effective curriculum as teachers focus their teaching on what is assessed.

Common Errors

- Failure to make adequate financial provision for key aspects of a national assessment, including report writing and dissemination.
- Failure to set up a national steering committee and to use it as a source of information and guidance during the course of the national assessment.
- Failure to gain government commitment to the process of national assessment, which is reflected in (a) a failure to identify key policy issues to be addressed at the design stage of the assessment, (b) the absence of a national steering committee, or (c) separate national assessments being carried out at the same time (often supported by external donors).
- Failure to involve key stakeholders (for example, teachers' representatives or teacher trainers) in planning the national assessment.
- Omission of a subgroup from the population assessed that is likely to seriously bias the results of the assessment (for example, students in private schools or students in small schools).
- Setting unrealistic test score targets (for example, 25 percent increase in scores over a four-year period).
- Allowing inadequate time for test development.

IMPLEMENTATION

Implementation covers a vast range of activities, from the development of appropriate assessment instruments, to the selection of the students who will respond to the instruments, to the administration of the instruments in schools.

Recommended Activities

- Describe in detail the content and cognitive skills of achievement and the background variables to be assessed.
- Entrust test development to personnel who are familiar with both curriculum standards and learning levels of students (especially practicing teachers).
- Use assessment instruments that adequately assess the knowledge and skills about which information is required and that will provide information on subdomains of knowledge or skills (for example, problem solving) rather than just an overall score.
- Develop clear and unambiguous test and questionnaire items, and present them in a clear and attractive manner.
- Ensure that adequate procedures are in place to assess the equivalence of language versions if translation of instruments is necessary.
- Pilot-test items, questionnaires, and manuals.
- Review items to identify ambiguities and possible bias relating to student characteristics (for example, gender, location, or ethnic group membership), and revise or delete if necessary.
- Proofread all materials carefully.
- Establish procedures to ensure the security of all national assessment materials (for example, tests and questionnaires) throughout the whole assessment process, so that materials do not fall into the hands of unauthorized people.
- Secure the services of a person or unit with sampling expertise.
- Specify the defined target population (the population from which a sample will actually be drawn—that is, the sampling frame) and the excluded population (for example, elements of the population

that are too difficult to reach or that would not be able to respond to the instrument). Precise data on excluded populations should be provided.

- Ensure that the proposed sample is representative and is of sufficient size to provide information on populations of interest with an acceptable level of error.
- Select members of the sample from the sampling frame according to known probabilities of selection.
- Follow a standard procedure when administering tests and questionnaires. Prepare an administration manual.
- Ensure that test administrators are thoroughly familiar with the contents of tests, questionnaires, and manuals and with administrative procedures.
- Prepare and implement a quality assurance mechanism to cover, among other things, test validity, sampling, printing, test administration, and data preparation.

Common Errors

- Assigning test development tasks to people who are unfamiliar with the likely levels of student performance (for example, academics), resulting in tests that are too difficult.
- Representing curriculum inadequately in tests, as indicated, for example, in failure to include important aspects of the curriculum.
- Failing to pilot-test items or pilot-testing on an unrepresentative sample of the population.
- Using an insufficient number of test items in the final version of the test.
- Failing to give a clear definition of the construct being assessed (for example, reading).
- Including an insufficient number of sample items for students who are unfamiliar with the testing format.
- Not encouraging students to seek clarification from the test supervisor before taking the test.
- Failing to give adequate notification to printers of tests, questionnaires, and manuals.
- Paying insufficient attention to proofreading tests, questionnaires, and administration manuals.

- Using inadequate or out-of-date national data on pupils and school numbers for sampling.
- Failing to carry out proper sampling procedures, including selecting a predetermined percentage of schools (for example, 5 percent).
- Providing inadequate training to test and questionnaire administrators.
- Allowing outside intervention (for example, principal sitting in the classroom) during test administration.
- Allowing students to sit close to each other during the assessment (encourages copying).
- Failing to establish a tradition of working outside normal work hours, if needed, to complete key tasks on time.

ANALYSIS

Statistical analyses organize, summarize, and interpret the data collected in schools. They should address the policy issues identified in the design of the national assessment.

Recommended Activities

- Secure competent statistical services.
- Prepare a codebook with specific directions for preparing data for analysis.
- Check and clean data to remove errors (for example, relating to numbers, out-of-range scores, and mismatches between data collected at different levels).
- Calculate sampling errors, taking into account complexities in the sample, such as stratification and clustering.
- Weight data so that the contribution of the various sectors of the sample to aggregate achievement scores reflects their proportions in the target population.
- Identify the percentage of students who met defined acceptable levels or standards.
- Analyze assessment data to identify factors that might account for variation in student achievement levels to help inform policy making.

- Analyze results by curriculum domain. Provide information on the subdomains of a curriculum area (for example, aspects of reading, mathematics).
- Recognize that a variety of measurement, curricular, and social factors may account for student performance.

Common Errors

- Using inappropriate statistical analyses, including failing to weight sample data in the analysis.
- Basing results on small numbers (for example, a minority of sampled teachers who might have responded to a particular question).
- Contrasting student performance in different curriculum areas, and claiming that students are doing better in one area on the basis of mean score differences.
- Failing to emphasize the arbitrary nature of selected test score cutoff points (for example, mastery versus nonmastery, pass versus fail), dichotomizing results, and failing to recognize the wide range of test scores in a group.
- Not reporting standard errors associated with individual statistics.
- Computing and publicizing school rankings on the basis of achievement test results without taking into account key contextual factors that contribute to the ranking. Different rankings emerge when school performances are compared using unadjusted performance scores, scores adjusted for contextual factors (for example, the percentage of students from poor socioeconomic backgrounds), and scores adjusted for earlier achievement.
- Inferring causation where it might not be justified (for example, attributing differences in learning achievement to one variable, such as private school administration or class size).
- Comparing test results over two time periods even though nonequivalent test items were used.
- Comparing test results over two time periods without reporting the extent to which important background conditions (for example, curriculum, enrollment, household income, or level of civil strife) might have changed in the interim. Although most education-related variables tend not to change rapidly over a short time (for example,

three to four years), some countries have introduced policies that have resulted in major changes in enrollment. Following the abolition of school fees, for example, the number of students enrolling in schools increased greatly in Malawi and Uganda.

- Limiting analysis in the main to a listing of mean scores of geographical or administrative regions.

REPORT WRITING

There is little point in carrying out a national assessment unless the findings are clearly reported with the needs of various stakeholders in mind.

Recommended Activities

- Prepare reports in a timely manner with the needs of clients in mind, and present them in a format that is readily understood by interested parties, especially those in a position to make decisions.
- Report results by gender and region, if sample design permits.
- Provide adequate information in the report or in a technical manual to allow for replication of the assessment.

Common Errors

- Writing overly technical reports.
- Failing to highlight a few main findings.
- Making recommendations in relation to a specific variable even though the analysis questioned the validity of the data on that variable.
- Failing to relate assessment results to curriculum, textbook, and teacher training issues.
- Not acknowledging that factors outside the control of the teacher and the school contribute to test score performance.
- Failing to recognize that differences between mean scores may not be statistically significant.
- Producing the report too late to influence relevant policy decisions.

- Doing an overextensive review of literature in the assessment report.
- Failing to publicize the key relevant messages of the report for separate stakeholder audiences.

DISSEMINATION AND USE OF FINDINGS

It is important that the results of national assessments are not left on policy makers' shelves but are communicated in appropriate language to all who can affect the quality of students' learning.

Recommended Activities

- Provide results to stakeholders, especially key policy makers and managers.
- Use the results where appropriate for policy making and to improve teaching and curricula.

Common Errors

- Ignoring the results when it comes to policy making.
- Among key stakeholders (for example, teacher trainers or curriculum personnel), failing to consider the implications of the national assessment findings.
- Among the national assessment team, failing to reflect on lessons learned and to take note of those lessons in follow-up assessments.

CHAPTER 6

INTERNATIONAL ASSESSMENTS OF STUDENT ACHIEVEMENT

In this chapter, we describe international assessments of students' educational achievement because they are used in many countries to provide data for a national assessment. First, we outline the main features of international assessments in terms of how they are similar to and differ from national assessments. Next, we describe growth in international assessment activity. Then the chapter identifies advantages of international assessments as well as problems associated with these assessments.

An international assessment of student achievement is similar in many ways to a national assessment. Both exercises use similar procedures (in instrument construction, sampling, scoring, and analysis). They also may have similar purposes: (a) to determine how well students are learning in the education system; (b) to identify particular strengths and weaknesses in the knowledge and skills that students have acquired; (c) to compare the achievements of subgroups in the population (for example, defined in terms of gender or location); or (d) to determine the relationship between student achievement and a variety of characteristics of the school learning environment and of homes and communities. Furthermore, both exercises may attempt to establish whether student achievements change over time (Kellaghan and Greaney 2004). In practice, however, why a country decides to participate in an international assessment is not always clear (Ferrer 2006).

The main advantage of an international assessment compared to a national assessment is that the former has as an objective to provide policy makers, educators, and the general public with information about their education system in relation to one or more other systems (Beaton and others 1999; Husén 1973; Postlethwaite 2004). This information is assumed to put pressure on policy makers and politicians to improve services. Furthermore, it is hoped that the information will contribute to a greater understanding of the factors (that vary from country to country) that contribute to differences in student achievement.

The curriculum areas that have attracted the largest participation rates in international studies over the years are reading comprehension, mathematics, and science. Studies have been carried out at primary- and secondary-school levels. Usually, a combination of grade and age is used to determine who will participate (for example, students in two adjacent grades that contain the largest proportions of 9-year-olds and 13-year-olds; students in the grade levels containing most 9-year-olds and most 14-year-olds; the upper of two adjacent grades with the most 9-year-olds). In yet another international study, students of a particular age were selected (15-year-olds).

The results of international assessments such as the Trends in International Mathematics and Science Study (TIMSS) and the Programme for International Student Assessment (PISA) and regional assessments can and have been used to prepare separate national reports on country-level performance. International databases can be accessed to carry out such analyses.

Countries vary considerably in the extent to which they rely on international and national assessment results for policy making. Many industrial countries conduct their own national assessments, as well as participating in international assessments. The United States has its own National Assessment of Educational Progress for grades 4, 8, and 12; it also participates in international assessments of achievement. Some industrial countries have participated in international assessments but do not conduct national assessments (for example, the Russian Federation and Germany). Similarly, some developing countries have used international assessments to provide their sole form of national assessment (Braun and Kanjee 2007). Many of the world's poorest countries have not taken part in international assessments or carried out national assessments, although the situation has changed in recent years.

GROWTH IN INTERNATIONAL ASSESSMENT ACTIVITY

International assessment activity began when a group of researchers met in 1958 to consider the possibility of undertaking a study of measured outcomes and their determinants within and between systems of education (Husén and Postlethwaite 1996). Since then, more than 60 countries have participated in international studies of achievement in one or more of a variety of curriculum areas: reading, mathematics, science, writing, literature, foreign languages, civic education, and computer literacy. The best-known international assessments are TIMSS (see B.1 in appendix B) and the Progress in International Reading Literacy Study (PIRLS) (see B.2 in appendix B) of the International Association for the Evaluation of Educational Achievement (IEA) and PISA (see B.3 in appendix B) of the Organisation for Economic Co-operation and Development (OECD). Regional assessments in reading and mathematics have been carried out in southern and eastern Africa (see C.1 in appendix C), in francophone Africa (see C.2 in appendix C), and in Latin America (see C.3 in appendix C). A number of features on which TIMSS and PISA differ are presented in table 6.1 (see also B.1 and B.3 in appendix B).

The number of countries participating in international studies has increased over the years. While typically fewer than 20 countries participated up to the 1980s, the IEA Reading Literacy Study attracted 32 countries in 1991. In 2003, 52 countries participated in TIMSS and 41 in PISA (30 member states of the OECD and 11 "partner" countries). Furthermore, international studies in recent years have accorded a major focus to monitoring performance over time. All three major current international assessments (TIMSS, PIRLS, and PISA) are administered on a cyclical basis and are now described as "trend" studies.

TABLE 6.1
Comparison of TIMSS and PISA

	TIMSS 2003	PISA 2003
Purposes	To provide comparative evidence on the extent to which students have mastered official school curriculum content in mathematics and science, which is common across a range of countries. To monitor changes in achievement levels over time. To monitor students' attitudes toward mathematics and science. To examine the relationship between a range of instructional and school factors and achievement. (Reading is covered in separate PIRLS assessment.)	To provide comparative evidence on the "yield" of the school system in the principal industrial countries, and to assess whether students can apply their knowledge and competencies in reading, mathematics, and science to real-world situations. To monitor changes in achievement levels and equity of learning outcomes over time. To monitor student approaches to learning and attitudes to mathematics, science, and reading. To provide a database for policy development.
Framework	Developed by content experts from some participating countries.	Developed by content experts from some participating countries.
Target population	Grades 4 and 8.	15-year-olds.
Curriculum appropriateness	Designed to assess official curriculum organized around recognized curriculum areas common to participating countries.	Designed to cover knowledge acquired both in school and out of school, defined in terms of overarching ideas and competencies applied to personal, educational, occupational, public, and scientific situations.

	TIMSS 2003	PISA 2003
Item content differences (mathematics, grade 8)	Grade 8, item distribution: • Number, 30% • Algebra, 25% • Data, 15% • Geometry, 15% • Measurement, 15%	Item distribution: • Number, 31.8% • Geometry, 21.2% • Statistics, 21.2% • Functions, 10.6% • Discrete math, 5.9% • Probability, 5.9% • Algebra, 3.5%
Cognitive processes	Grade 8: • Solving routine problems 40% • Using concepts 20% • Knowing facts and procedures 15% • Reasoning 25%	Mathematics, overarching ideas: • Quantity • Space and shape • Change and relationships • Uncertainty Item distribution: • Connection, 47% • Reproduction, 31% • Reflection, 22%
Item types (mathematics)	About two-thirds being multiple-choice items, with the remainder being constructed-response or open-ended items.	About one-third being multiple-choice items, with the remainder generally being closed (one possible correct response) or open (more than one possible correct response) constructed-response items.
Frequency	Every four years: equal emphasis on mathematics and science in each cycle.	Every three years: extensive coverage of one domain (subject) every nine years (reading in 2000, mathematics in 2003, and science in 2006), plus less extensive coverage of the other two every three years.
Geographical coverage	48 countries: 20 high-income, 26 middle-income, and 2 low-income countries.	30 OECD countries as well as 11 other countries.
Analysis	Four benchmark levels and a mean score, which are based on all participating countries.	Seven mathematics proficiency levels and a mean score, which are based on OECD countries.

Source: TIMSS and PISA frameworks; U.S. National Center for Education Statistics n.d.; World Development Indicators database.

Participation by nonindustrial countries in international studies has generally been low. Nevertheless, in line with the general increase in the number of countries that have taken part in international studies, the number of nonindustrial countries has increased over the years. TIMSS attracted the largest numbers in 2003 (seven from Africa) and 2007 (six from Africa). As was the case generally in international studies, nonindustrial countries have shown a greater interest in taking part in studies of mathematics and reading than in studies of other curriculum areas.

Recent growth in participation in international studies can be attributed to globalization, to a movement in health and education to benchmark services against those in other countries, and to interest in global mandates. Some research evidence supports the view that educational quality (in particular those aspects of it represented by mathematics and science achievements) plays an important role in economic growth, though it is not entirely consistent across countries or over time (Coulombe, Tremblay, and Marchand 2004; Hanushek and Kimko 2000; Hanushek and Wössmann 2007; Ramirez and others 2006). Whatever the reason, education policy around the world has increasingly focused on the need to monitor aggregate student achievement in an international context.

ADVANTAGES OF INTERNATIONAL ASSESSMENTS

A variety of reasons have been proposed to encourage countries to participate in an international assessment of student achievement. Perhaps the most obvious is that international studies provide a comparative framework in which to assess student achievement and curricular provision in a country and to devise procedures to address perceived deficiencies (Štraus 2005). By comparing results from different countries, countries can use assessment results to help define what is achievable, how achievement is distributed, and what relationships exist between average achievement and its distribution. For example, can high average achievement coexist with narrow disparities in performance? Results from PISA suggest that it can.

Data on achievement provide only limited information. It has been argued that an advantage of international studies is that they can capitalize on the variability that exists across education systems, thereby broadening the range of conditions that can be studied beyond those operating in any one country (Husén 1973). On this basis, the analysis of data collected in these studies routinely considers associations between achievement and a wide range of contextual variables. The range of variables considered includes curriculum content, time spent on school work, teacher training, class size, and organization of the education system. Clearly, the value of international studies is enhanced to the extent that they provide researchers and policy makers with information that suggests hypotheses about the reasons students differ in their achievements from country to country. The studies also provide a basis for the evaluation of policy and practices.

International assessments have the potential to bring to light the concepts for understanding education that have been overlooked in a country (for example, in defining literacy or in conceptualizing curricula in terms of intention, implementation, and achievement; see, for example, Elley 2005). The assessments can also help identify and lead to questioning of assumptions that may be taken for granted (for example, the value of comprehensive compared to selective education, smaller class sizes being associated with higher achievement, or grade repetition benefiting students).

International studies are likely to attract the attention of the media and of a broad spectrum of stakeholders, such as politicians, policy makers, academics, teachers, and the public. Differences between countries in levels of achievement are obvious in the descriptive statistics that are provided in reports of the studies. Indeed, those differences are usually highlighted in "league tables" in which countries are ranked in terms of their mean level of achievement. The comparative data provided in these studies have more "shock value" than the results of a national assessment. Poor results can encourage debate, which, in turn, may provide politicians and other policy makers with a rationale for increased budgetary support for the education sector, particularly if poor results are associated with a lower level of expenditure on education.

An important feature of an international assessment is that it provides data that individual countries can use to carry out within-country analyses for what becomes, in effect, a national assessment report. This practice is followed by countries that participate in PISA (see B.3 in appendix B) and SACMEQ (see C.1 in appendix C). The practice is enhanced if, in addition to the data collected for the international study, data that relate to issues of specific interest or concern in individual countries are also collected.

Participation in international assessments has a number of practical advantages, particularly for countries that do not have the capacity in their universities to develop the kinds of skills needed in national assessments. First, a central agency may carry out national-level analyses that can be used in individual country reports. Second, studies may contribute to the development of local capacity in a variety of technical activities: sampling, defining achievements, developing tests, analyzing statistics, and writing reports. Third, staffing requirements and costs (for example, for instrument development, data cleaning, and analysis) may be lower than in national assessments because costs are shared with other countries.

A study of the effect of TIMSS on the teaching and learning of mathematics and science in participating countries provides evidence of the variety of activities that an international study can spawn (Robitaille, Beaton, and Plomp 2000):

- TIMSS results featured in parliamentary discussions about planned changes in education policy (Japan).
- The minister for education established a mathematics and science task force (New Zealand).
- The president directed that a "rescue package" be implemented to improve performance in science and mathematics (in which teacher training would receive particular attention) (the Philippines).
- National benchmarks were established in literacy and numeracy (Australia).
- Results contributed to the development of new educational standards in mathematics and science (Russian Federation).
- Results helped change the nature of public discussions in the field of education from opinion-based discussions to fact-based discussions (Switzerland).

- Results led to the development of instructional materials that are based on analysis of the common misconceptions and errors of students in their response to TIMSS tasks (Canada).
- Results accelerated changes in revision of curricula (Czech Republic; Singapore).
- TIMSS results were identified as one of a number of factors influencing policy changes in mathematics education (England).
- Committees were formed to revise mathematics and science curricula (Kuwait).
- New topics were added to the mathematics curriculum (Romania).
- New content was introduced to the mathematics and science curriculum relating to real-life situations (Spain).
- Results helped highlight the need to improve the balance between pure mathematics and mathematics in context (Sweden).
- TIMSS findings highlighted beliefs about gender differences and negative attitudes to science and mathematics and were used as a basis for curriculum reform and teachers' professional development (Republic of Korea).
- Results influenced the outcome of discussions about improving the organization of, and emphasis in, teacher education (Iceland).
- TIMSS results led to taking steps to strengthen teacher professional development in mathematics and science (Norway; the United States).
- A centralized examination system was established, partly in response to TIMSS results (Latvia).
- TIMSS findings influenced major changes in teaching, school and class organization, teacher education, and target-setting for schools (Scotland).
- TIMSS findings affected educational research, standards development, curriculum document development, teacher studies, mathematics and science teaching methodologies, and textbook development (Slovak Republic).

The results of analyses of PISA data have led to the following:

- Cast doubt on the value of extensive use of computers in the classroom to improve achievement.
- Highlighted the fact that level of national expenditure on education is not associated with achievement (among participating countries).

- Prompted general policy debate on education (Germany).
- Contributed to the development of the secondary-school science curriculum (Ireland).
- Emphasized the complexity of the relationship between socio-economic status and reading achievement across countries.
- Underscored the link between achievement and school types and curriculum tracking within schools.
- Supported the notion that public and private schools tend to have the same effects for the same kinds of pupils but that private government-dependent schools are relatively more effective for pupils from lower socioeconomic levels.
- Stressed the need for intensive language and reading programs for foreign-born students to help boost achievement (Switzerland).

PROBLEMS WITH INTERNATIONAL ASSESSMENTS

Despite obvious advantages, a number of problems associated with international assessments merit consideration before countries decide to participate in one (see Kellaghan 1996).

First, an assessment procedure that will adequately measure the outcomes of a variety of curricula is difficult to design. Although curricula across the world have common elements, particularly at the primary-school level, considerable differences between countries also exist in what is taught, when it is taught, and what standards of achievement are expected.

South Africa's review of TIMSS items shows that only 18 percent of the science items matched the national curriculum of grade 7, while 50 percent matched the grade 8 curriculum (Howie and Hughes 2000). The greater the difference between the curricula and levels of achievement of countries participating in an international assessment, the more difficult it is to devise an assessment procedure that will suit all countries, and the more doubtful is the validity of any inferences that are made about comparative achievements.

We would expect an achievement test that is based on the content of a national curriculum to provide a more valid measure of curriculum mastery than would one that was designed to serve as a common denominator of the curricula offered in 30 to 40 countries. For example, a national curriculum authority and the designers of an international assessment might assign quite different weights of importance to a skill such as drawing inferences from a text. A national assessment, as opposed to an international assessment, can also test curricular aspects that are unique to individual countries.

Devising a common assessment instrument is more difficult for some curriculum areas (for example, science and social studies) than for others (for example, reading). In the case of science, for example, achievement patterns have been found to be more heterogeneous than in mathematics. Furthermore, a greater number of factors are required to account for student performance differences in science than in mathematics. Thus, a science test that would be appropriate for a variety of education systems is difficult to envisage.

A second problem with international studies is that—although early studies had the ambitious aim of capitalizing on the variation that exists in education systems to assess the relative importance of a variety of school resources and instructional processes—this goal, in practice, turned out to be very difficult to achieve. Because the relative effect of variables depends on the context in which they are embedded, practices associated with high achievement in one country cannot be assumed to show a similar relationship in another. In fact, the strength of correlations between background factors and achievement has been found to vary from country to country (see, for example, OECD and UNESCO Institute for Statistics 2003; Wilkins, Zembylas, and Travers 2002). Particular difficulties exist when developing countries are involved in a study designed for industrial countries because socio-economic factors in such countries can differ very much from those that prevail in industrial countries and can include poverty, nutritional and health factors, and poor educational infrastructure and resourcing.

Third, the populations and samples of students participating in international assessments may not be strictly comparable. For example, differences in performance might arise because countries differ in the extent to which categories of students are removed from mainstream classes and so may be excluded from an assessment (for example, students in special programs or students in schools in which the language of instruction differs from the language of the assessment).

The problem is most obvious where (a) age of enrolling in schools, (b) retention, and (c) dropout rates differ from one country to another and is particularly relevant in studies in which industrial and developing countries participate. In some developing countries, large proportions of students have dropped out well before the end of the period of compulsory schooling. Whereas primary school net enrollment ratios for Western Europe and North America are almost 100 percent, the ratios for countries in Sub-Saharan Africa are, on average, less than 60 percent (UNESCO 2002). Patterns of early dropout can differ from country to country. In Latin American and Arab countries, boys are more likely than girls not to complete grade 5; the reverse is true in some African countries (for example, Guinea and Mozambique). Sampling problems for TIMSS appeared in the Republic of Yemen, where several schools did not have grade 4 classes and where one school for nomadic children could not be located.

Similar comparability problems can arise in a national assessment. For example, the differential performance of students in states in India has been attributed to differential survival rates (see A.1 in appendix A).

Fourth, because variation in test score performance is an important factor if one is (a) to describe adequately the achievements of students in the education system and (b) to determine correlates of achievement, carefully designed national tests must ensure a relatively wide distribution of test scores. However, many items in international assessments have been too difficult for students from less industrial countries, resulting in restricted test score variance. This result is reflected in the data presented in table 6.2, which are based on a selection of countries that participated in TIMSS 2003.

The data show the percentage of grade 8 students who reached levels or benchmarks of performance when compared to all students who took the test. Seven percent of all those who took the mathematics test achieved the "advanced" international benchmark, 23 percent the "high" benchmark, one-half the "intermediate" benchmark, and roughly three-quarters the "low" benchmark. In sharp contrast, 2 percent of Ghanaian students achieved the "intermediate" benchmark and 9 percent achieved the "low" benchmark. Zero percent achieved the "advanced" and "high" international benchmarks.

TABLE 6.2
Percentage of Students Reaching TIMSS International Benchmarks in Mathematics, Grade 8: High- and Low-Scoring Countries

Countries	Advanced[a]	High[a]	Intermediate[a]	Low[a]
Singapore	44	77	93	99
Chinese Taipei	38	66	85	96
Korea, Rep. of	35	70	90	98
International average	**7**	**23**	**49**	**74**
Philippines	0	3	14	39
Bahrain	0	2	17	51
South Africa	0	2	6	10
Tunisia	0	1	15	55
Morocco	0	1	10	42
Botswana	0	1	7	32
Saudi Arabia	0	0	3	19
Ghana	0	0	2	9

Source: Mullis and others 2004, 64.
a. Definitions used in TIMSS 2003: *Advanced:* Students can organize information, make generalizations, solve nonroutine problems, and draw and justify conclusions from data. *High:* Students can apply their understanding and knowledge in a wide variety of relatively complex situations. *Intermediate:* Students can apply basic mathematical knowledge in straightforward solutions. *Low:* Students have some basic mathematical knowledge.

Similarly, on PISA 2003, the limited use of the assessment for internal policy making was underscored by the lack of test score variance in a number of participating countries; the majority of 15-year-olds in Brazil, Indonesia, and Tunisia scored below Level 1. (Level 2 has been suggested as a minimum requirement for students entering the world of work and further education.) Clearly, the information that those studies provide for policy makers and decision makers on the range of student achievements in these education systems is limited. Furthermore, because of the limited variance in achievement, correlations between achievement and background or school variables would throw little light on the factors that contribute to achievement.

Fifth, a problem arises when the primary focus in reporting the results of an international assessment is on the ranking of countries in terms of the average scores of their students, which are usually the main interest of media. Rankings in themselves tell us nothing about the many factors that may underlie differences between countries in performance. Furthermore, rankings can be misleading when the statistical significance of mean differences in achievement is ignored. A country's rank can vary depending on the countries that participate, an important consideration when rankings over time are compared. Thus, for example, if the number of traditionally high-achieving countries decreases and the number of traditionally low-achieving countries increases, a country's ranking may increase without necessarily implying an improvement in achievement.

Sixth, poor performance in an international assessment (as well as in a national assessment) can carry with it some political risks for key officials associated with the delivery of education, including ministers and secretaries of education ministries. The risk is likely to be greater when the international rank of a country is lower than that of a traditional rival country. In some countries in which data were collected, officials refused to allow the results to be included in between-country published comparisons. (IEA no longer permits participating countries to opt out of comparisons.) Obtaining comparative data for neighboring countries or countries within a region would seem more appropriate than obtaining data for countries across the world that differ greatly in their level of socioeconomic development. An example of this approach is found in Latin America and the Caribbean, where 13 countries jointly carried out an assessment of basic competencies in language and mathematics in 1997 (see C.3 in appendix C). The SACMEQ assessments in southern and eastern Africa that were carried out under the auspices of a network of ministries in the 1990s also allowed for international comparisons at a regional level (see C.1 in appendix C).

Seventh, the demands of meeting deadlines may prove very difficult in countries that lack administrative personnel and that have to cope with a poor communications infrastructure (see box 6.1). The time allowed for carrying out various tasks (for example, printing or distributing booklets), which are associated with an international assessment and which may be deemed reasonable in industrial countries, may be insufficient given the range of basic problems— including poor communication systems—that exist in many developing countries.

BOX 6.1

South Africa's Experience with International Assessments

South Africa's experience with TIMSS underlines the problems facing implementers of international assessments. Deadlines imposed by organizers can be difficult, if not impossible, to meet in situations where mail service, telephone service, or funds for travel to schools are inadequate.

Other problems include lack of accurate population data on schools; poor management skills; insufficient attention to detail, especially in editing, coding, and data capture; lack of funding to support project workers; and difficulty in securing quality printing on time. Instructions to test administrators (for example, to walk up and down the aisle) are obviously inappropriate when classrooms do not have an aisle.

Source: Howie 2000.

Finally, substantial costs are associated with participation in an international study. A country participating in TIMSS for grade 8 was expected to pay US$40,000 in addition to all costs associated with printing, distribution, test administration, data entry, and scoring. National assessments, of course, also have considerable associated costs.

CHAPTER 7

CONCLUSION

Readers who have persevered to this point should be familiar with the main features of national and international assessments, with how the assessments are similar and how they differ, with the reasons for engaging in an assessment, and with the problems to look out for in the process. Readers also should have a general understanding of the main activities involved, including identification of key policy issues, construction of instruments, selection of schools and of students to represent the education system, analysis of data to describe student achievements and their correlates, and communication of findings to a range of audiences. Specialized knowledge and skills are required for all those tasks.

If the reader is a senior policy maker or manager in a ministry of education, he or she is unlikely to possess any of the specialized knowledge or skills that are involved in the details of executing a national assessment. This lack does not mean that he or she does not have a crucial role to play in an assessment—from its initiation and general design, to facilitating its implementation, and to interpreting and applying its findings. In this chapter, we pay particular attention to the role of the policy maker or manager in the development and institutionalization of national assessment activity and in the optimal use of assessment findings.

Senior policy makers or managers who are in a position to make decisions about whether to undertake a national assessment (or to participate in an international assessment) should be convinced that the information the assessment will provide will be useful in identifying problems in the education system and in informing policy and practice to address those problems. Their commitment is likely to be enhanced if the assessment meets five conditions.

First, the student achievements that are assessed are considered important outcomes of schooling and adequately reflect the curriculum. Second, the instrument used in the assessment has the potential to provide diagnostic information about aspects of student achievement, in particular, strengths and weaknesses in the profile of achievement. Third, the method of sampling (if the assessment is sample based) ensures that the data that are collected adequately represent the achievements of the education system as a whole (or a clearly identified part of it). Fourth, appropriate analyses are used to identify and describe the main features of the data, including relationships between significant variables. Fifth, the technical aspects of the assessment meet current professional standards in areas such as test development, sampling, and statistical analysis.

All those activities require considerable resources and political support. For example, the policy maker or manager has a crucial role in ensuring that the knowledge and skills that are required to design, manage, and interpret a national assessment are available. In many countries, they will not be available locally and will have to be developed specifically to carry out an assessment. This development will require initial long- or short-term training programs. Following those programs, provision should be made for increasing the technical skills of those involved in the administration of a national assessment on a regular basis through in-country training programs, attendance at professional meetings, and more long-term graduate study.

In some countries, national assessment activity seems to operate on the fringes of the education system, divorced from the normal structure and processes of policy and decision making. In this situation, no guarantee exists that the information obtained in an assessment will be used to guide policy or that national assessments will be carried out in the future to monitor how achievement might change over time. To address those issues, national assessment activity should become a normal part of the functioning of the education system. This activity will require active involvement of some senior policy makers in the overall design of the assessment and in either participation in, or representation on, the national steering committee. It will also require an adequate budget and a decision about the location of the activity, which will vary from country to country depending on local circumstances.

Long-term government commitment is very important in building a strong institutional base for carrying out regular national assessments. It can permit an agency to recruit and train individuals with key expertise in areas such as test development, sampling, and statistical analysis. Weak commitment can be reflected in a pattern of assigning national assessment to different agencies, a strategy that does little or nothing to build up much-needed technical expertise in the relevant disciplines. In more than one country, multiple agencies have carried out separate national assessments, using a range of approaches of limited value for education policy making.

In some instances, government commitment can be increased when a unit within the ministry—supported by a line item in the education budget—carries out the assessment. In Chile, for example, government commitment and responsiveness to the results of the Sistema de Medición de la Calidad de la Educación (SIMCE) increased when the national assessment was transferred from a university to the ministry. Annual assessment, timely reporting of results, and an appreciation of the value of the results for policy making helped strengthen SIMCE's legitimacy, institutionalize its work, and ensure further long-term government commitment and support. In a number of other Latin American countries, assessment institutes, which are independent of the ministry of education, have succeeded in developing a record of competency and autonomy, thus conducting assessments with considerable flexibility and consistency (Ferrer 2006).

Institutionalization in itself is not enough, although it probably would go some way toward ensuring that a situation does not arise in which national assessment findings do not reach key government personnel. A need also exists to invest effort in devising procedures to communicate findings to stakeholders inside and outside the ministry.

Apart from government officials, national assessment findings are relevant to the work of curriculum developers, examination bodies, teacher educators, and teachers in their everyday practice in schools. Addressing the information needs of this variety of audiences requires production of a number of reports and adoption of various dissemination strategies. Strategies should identify potential users (key institutions and individuals) and their level of technical expertise. A technical report is required (that provides sufficient information to allow a replication of the study), but technical data also need to be translated into forms that are accessible to nontechnical users, which may be presented in a summary report (for example, for the public) or in a more detailed report for policy makers, which can indicate, for example, (a) if the system is underserving any particular group, (b) if gaps warrant remedial action, and (c) if factors associated with superior performance can be identified.

In many countries, policy making tends to be influenced by political priorities and the perceptions of ministers and senior officials. It is frequently prompted by personal experiences and anecdotal information, as well as by political pressure. Far too rarely is it informed by the results of an analysis of valid and reliable data on the functioning of the education system, such as can be provided by a well-designed and implemented national assessment.

Policy makers should provide leadership in ensuring that objective, reliable evidence on the functioning of the education system provided by the national assessment is used to help improve the overall quality of policy making. They can do so by examining and reflecting on the relevance of the national assessment results for policy making in areas such as gender and regional equity, provision of educational materials in schools, teacher qualifications, and provision of in-service courses for teachers. They can reflect on whether changes introduced since the previous national assessment appear to have affected student achievement. They can encourage and support providers of teacher education (preservice and in-service) courses to study the findings and adjust current practices where evidence indicates the need for adjustment. Policy makers can also advise a curriculum authority on changes in curriculum content when evidence clearly indicates that students find the material much too easy or, more likely, too difficult.

Close involvement of policy makers at the outset in the overall design of the assessment, and again when the assessment is complete to discuss the relevance of results can help ensure that they come to appreciate the value of a national assessment. Over time, it may be hoped that the policy makers will come to regard a national assessment as a key policy-making instrument.

Brief descriptions of national assessment practices in nine countries are presented in appendix A. The descriptions are not exhaustive, and the cases are not presented as perfect models of good practice. Several of them, in fact, are defective in a number of technical aspects. They do, however, reveal similarities and differences in approach that are of interest. Similarities are reflected in the fact that—in all countries—assessments were carried out in language/literacy and mathematics/numeracy at one or more primary-grade levels. In all countries, assessments that were based on samples were carried out. In Chile and Uruguay, assessments in which the population of schools participated were also carried out.

Differences between countries are reflected in the frequency of assessment, which varied from one to four years. The agency responsible for implementation of the assessment also varied and included the ministry of education, a government-supported research institute, and a national examinations board. Considerable nonnational support was available to the implementing agency in several countries. In at least two countries (Chile and South Africa), the implementation agency changed between assessments.

The way in which student achievement was described varied from citing the mean and distribution of the number of items to which students responded correctly, to determining the percentage of students whose performance reached "expected" standards or the percentage scoring at varying levels of "proficiency." Methods of analysis also varied considerably, probably a reflection of the technical capacity of national assessment teams. Sophisticated analytic approaches were used in some countries (for example, the United States and Vietnam).

The use of results from assessments seemed to vary a good deal, although this conclusion is not certain because not a great deal of information is available in most countries on the extent to which results have been disseminated or have been effective in contributing to policy formation. As well as describing gender differences, some countries have used the results of a national assessment to support the following actions:

- Provide policy recommendations for the education sector (Sri Lanka, Vietnam).
- Document regional disparities in achievement (Nepal, South Africa, Sri Lanka).
- Design a major in-service program for teachers (Uruguay).
- Provide financial and other forms of support to low-scoring schools (Chile).
- Bring strengths and weaknesses in student achievements to the notice of teachers (Uganda).
- Describe changes in the achievements of minority-group students over time (United States).
- Suggest a reduction in the emphasis on algebra and geometry in the curriculum (Bhutan).

Those involved in the design of a national assessment might like to consider a number of somewhat unusual practices that are features of the assessments described in appendix A:

- Launching a public-awareness campaign prior to the assessment (Chile).
- Collecting data in conjunction with data on student achievement to monitor the extent to which school facilities improve over time (Vietnam).
- Administering the achievement test to teachers as well as to students (India, Vietnam).
- Working closely with teacher unions to carry out the assessment (Uruguay).

Appendix B provides descriptions of the main features of three current, large-scale, international studies that span the globe. Those studies focus on reading/literacy, mathematics/numeracy, and science—three areas of knowledge and skill that would probably be regarded as "core" in students' education in all countries. All three studies are also concerned with monitoring student achievement over time.

The level of technical competence in international studies is very high, and countries can improve their knowledge and skill by participating. Many countries, as we have seen, also use the data collected in an international assessment to carry out national-level analyses, in effect using the international assessment as a national assessment. This procedure can be enriched if national-level background information is collected in addition to that required in the international study.

The design of international studies is very similar to the design of a national assessment, except that cognizance has to be taken of the fact that the assessment will be carried out in a number of countries. Thus, assessment instruments may not be equally appropriate in all countries, either because they do not adequately represent school curricula, which vary from country to country, or because they do not adequately reflect the range of student achievements, which can vary enormously from country to country. Two approaches have been adopted to address variation in school curricula. In the Trends in International Mathematics and Science Study (TIMSS) (B.1 in appendix B), as in earlier studies carried out under the auspices of the International Association for the Evaluation of Educational Achievement, tests are developed in a consensus-building exercise among participating countries in which common elements of their curricula are included in tests. The approach of the Programme for International Student Assessment (PISA) (B.3 in appendix B) has been not to base assessment instruments on an analysis of curricula, but to use "expert" opinion to determine the knowledge and skills that 15-year-olds should have acquired near the end of compulsory education if they are to participate fully in society.

The fact that student achievement is related to countries' economic development means that assessments designed for industrial countries (such as TIMSS and PISA) are unlikely to provide a satisfactory description of achievement in a developing country. Regional studies for less industrial countries have been created to address this issue, and three such studies—two in Africa and one in Latin America—are described in appendix C. Those studies act as both national and international assessments.

APPENDIX A

COUNTRY CASE STUDIES

A.1. India

Purpose. An assessment was developed to help the government of India provide baseline data on the quality of education for each of its states. The assessment was part of the government's Sarva Shiksha Abhiyan (SSA) program, which aimed to achieve universal enrollment up to the completion of elementary education by 2010. Earlier large-scale achievement assessments had been carried out in designated school districts as part of the government's District Primary Education Project (Prakash, Gautam, and Bansal 2000). Mean scores for mathematics and language were compared by district, subject area, and grade level. The assessment concluded that students were better in language and that the average achievement in the sample of older students was not as impressive as that of students in lower grades. The majority of differences within districts between boys and girls in mathematics and in language were not statistically significant. In addition to this district-level assessment, a large-scale assessment was carried out in 22 states in the early 1990s (Shukla and others 1994).

Frequency. Every three years.

Grades. The grade 5 assessment was administered in 2001–02. Grade 3 and the terminal grade for elementary education (which varies from state to state) were also assessed.

Achievements assessed. Language and mathematics.

Who did it? National Council of Research and Training, Delhi, with the support of the District Institutes of Education, which supervised the data collection.

Sample or population. Sample.

Analysis. Reported grade 5 scores for each state in terms of the percentage of items answered correctly.

Use of results. Grade 5 results showed small gender and rural-urban gaps in achievement levels. The data will be used to monitor changes in levels of educational achievement and to identify educational and noneducational factors that may help account for differences in student achievement.

Interesting points. An earlier large-scale 22-state assessment administered the same test to teachers and students. In one state with very low mean student scores, only 1 of 70 teachers who took the test answered all 40 arithmetic items correctly. Among the teachers, 10 percent answered fewer than half the items correctly (Shukla and others 1994).

The national assessment will be used to help monitor the effect of the SSA initiative. Unlike most other national assessments, scores are reported in terms of overall percentage of items answered correctly. States with particularly poor achievement levels are expected to receive special attention. Some states with strong education traditions in terms of school participation rates (for example, Kerala and Himachal Pradash) recorded relatively low mean scores on the grade 5 assessment, while some of the states with relatively low school participation rates (for example, Bihar, Orissa, and West Bengal) scored higher. This outcome, which was also reported in the earlier 22-state assessment, is explained by the fact that in the latter states, the samples of students taking the tests tended to be "survivors" in the education system; many of the less advantaged students in terms of home background and ability levels would have dropped out of school by grade 5.

Source: India, National Council of Educational Research and Training, Department of Educational Measurement and Evaluation 2003.

A.2. Vietnam

Purpose. To measure the quality of education with a particular focus on student achievement at the primary level.

Frequency. Previous small-scale assessments had been carried out between 1998 and 2000 at grades 3 and 5, but they were inappropriate for providing benchmark information for monitoring trends over time.

Grade. 5.

Achievements assessed. Vietnamese reading and mathematics in 2001.

Instruments. Achievement tests; pupil, teacher, and school questionnaires.

Who did it? Ministry of Education and Training supported by other national agencies and an international team supported by the World Bank and the Department for International Development of the United Kingdom.

Sample or population. Sample was designed to be representative of the national population and populations in each of 61 provinces.

Analysis. Analyses included cross-tabulations of achievement data and school data by region, correlates of achievement, factor analysis, item response modeling of test item data, and hierarchical linear modeling for identification of factors associated with achievement.

Use of results. Government officials made 40 policy recommendations that were based on the overall results.

Interesting points. Tests included items from the 1991 International Association for the Evaluation of Educational Achievement Reading Literacy Study (Elley 1992, 1994) that were used to compare results with other countries. The same tests were administered to teachers and students; 12 percent of students scored higher than 30 percent of teachers. Fewer than 3 percent of schools had obligatory school resources (for example, library, piped water). More than 80 percent of pupils were in classrooms that had minimal resources (writing board, chalk, and so on) while 10 percent were being taught by teachers who had not completed secondary school.

Six levels of proficiency were established according to students' performance on the reading test:

- *Level 1*. Matches text at word or sentence level aided by pictures. Restricted to a limited range of vocabulary linked to pictures.
- *Level 2*. Locates text expressed in short repetitive sentences and can deal with text unaided by pictures. Text is limited to short sentences and phrases with repetitive patterns.
- *Level 3*. Reads and understands longer passages. Can search backward or forward through text for information. Understands paraphrasing. Expanding vocabulary enables understanding of sentences with some complex structure.
- *Level 4*. Links information from different parts of the text. Selects and connects text to derive and to infer different possible meanings.
- *Level 5*. Links inferences and identifies an author's intention from information stated in different ways, in different text types, and in documents where the information is not explicit.
- *Level 6*. Combines text with outside knowledge to infer various meanings, including hidden meanings. Identifies an author's purposes, attitudes, values, beliefs, motives, unstated assumptions, and arguments.

There was considerable variation in the level of student performance on both the reading and mathematics tests. For example, far fewer students attained the two highest levels of reading in Ha Giang and Tien than in Da Nang (table A.2.1). The relationship between teacher characteristics and students' scores was examined after taking home background into account (table A.2.2).

Source: World Bank 2004.

TABLE A.2.1

Percentages and Standard Errors of Pupils at Different Skill Levels in Reading

Province	Unit indicator	Level 1	Level 2	Level 3	Level 4	Level 5	Level 6
Ha Giang	Percentage	7.5	22.1	27.4	18.7	18.5	5.7
	SE	1.66	3.23	3.06	2.97	3.07	2.09
Tien Giang	Percentage	2.8	13.4	28.8	20.2	22.4	12.5
	SE	0.7	2.0	2.49	1.8	2.46	2.78
Da Nang	Percentage	0.8	5.7	15.4	21.3	32.9	24.1
	SE	0.34	0.88	1.79	1.89	1.98	3.23
Vietnam	Percentage	4.6	14.4	23.1	20.2	24.5	13.1
	SE	0.17	0.28	0.34	0.27	0.39	0.41

Source: World Bank 2004, vol. 2, table 2.3.
Note: SE = standard error.

TABLE A.2.2

Relationship between Selected Teacher Variables and Mathematics Achievement

Teacher variable	Simple correlation	Partial correlation, after taking pupil's home background into account
Sex of teacher[a]	0.17	0.14
Academic education	0.08	0.04
Subject knowledge of mathematics	0.29	0.25
Classified as "excellent teacher"	0.18	0.13
Classroom resources	0.24	0.15
Number of hours preparing and marking	0.00	0.01
Frequency of meeting with parents	0.05	0.04
Number of inspection visits	0.13	0.11

Source: World Bank 2004, vol. 2, table 4.38.
Note: Correlations greater than 0.02 are statistically significant.
a. Pupils taught by female teachers scored higher.

A.3. Uruguay

Purpose. The national assessment aimed to identify (a) the extent to which primary school graduates had developed a "fundamental understanding" of language and mathematics, and (b) the sociocultural factors that may have a bearing on student achievement. The assessment emphasized professional development, which included diagnosing learning problems, giving teachers information about student performance, and helping them improve teaching and evaluation. The assessment also aimed to use the data from the tests and questionnaires to improve school conditions.

Frequency and grade. Grade 6 (every three years) in 1996, 1999, 2002, and 2005. In addition, grades 1, 2, and 3 were assessed for teacher development purposes in 2001. Grade 9 was tested in 1999 and grade 12 in 2003. Since 2003, 15-year-olds are being assessed as part of the Programme for International Student Assessment (PISA).

Achievements assessed. Mathematics (problem solving) and reading comprehension in grade 6; mathematics, language, and natural and social sciences in grades 9 and 12.

Instruments. Achievement tests; parent, teacher, and principal questionnaires.

Who did it? Early on, Unidad de Medición de Resultados Educativos (UMRE), a unit created as part of a World Bank–financed project, was responsible for the national assessment at grade 6 while Programa de Modernización de la Educación Secundaria y Formación Docente (MESyFOD), an Inter-American Bank–funded project, was responsible for the national assessment at the secondary level. Since 2001, the assessment activities have been unified and institutionalized under the Gerencia de Investigación y Evaluación (Research and Assessment Division), part of the National Administration for Public Education. Finance is provided by international donor agencies.

Sample or population. Population and sample of grade 6 students, excluding very small rural schools; population of grade 9 students; sample of grades 1, 2, 3, and 12; sample for PISA assessments.

Analysis. UMRE used 60 percent correct as an index of adequacy of pupil performance. Individual school scores were compared to the national average, to the departmental or regional average, and to schools serving students from similar socioeconomic backgrounds. Achievement test data were related to background factors.

Use of results. Results were used mainly by teachers, principals, and the school inspectorate. The government used the results to identify schools for special support and for large-scale, in-service, teacher-training programs. National-level results were widely publicized. Forty days after testing and before the end of the school year, participating schools received a confidential report with aggregate school results presented item by item. The reports did not include individual student results or results disaggregated by classroom. UMRE (a) produced teaching guides to help address perceived weaknesses in language and mathematics and organized in-service, teacher-training programs for schools in disadvantaged areas, (b) prepared reports for supervisory personnel, and (c) held workshops for inspectors that drew on the test results. Tests were made available to schools other than the sampled ones. Every school received a report of national averages for each competency tested. Nontested schools were sent norms for comparative purposes. Close to 80 percent of those schools administered the tests and compared their results to supplied national norms. Inspectors held their own workshops to develop an understanding of the results, to appreciate the effect of social deprivation on student learning outcomes, and to suggest courses of action to enhance educational quality.

Interesting points. Initially the teachers' union at the primary level was strongly opposed to the national assessment. In particular, it opposed the publication of individual school results. Eventually, the union was won over by the government's agreement not to publish results for individual schools or teachers, but to allow the results to be used for diagnostic purposes. Only aggregate data were to be published. In addition, the government invited teachers to participate (a) in the groups that planned the assessment and (b) in other advisory groups. Teachers were also heavily involved in test development. To date, little opposition has arisen to formal assessment of this type at the primary level. There has been a general acceptance that teachers or schools will not be penalized for poor test results. The secondary teachers' union has not been very supportive of the assessment and has adopted a wait-and-see attitude. The acceptance by teachers of the UMRE initiative and of the results is attributable to confidentiality of test results, prompt reporting, contextualization of test scores by sociocultural background, and acknowledgment that student outcomes depend on a combination of factors (including household, school, community, and teacher variables).

Although governments in some countries are seeking ways to hold schools and teachers accountable for student outcomes, Uruguay takes a different approach. The state takes responsibility for promoting an enabling environment to help achieve equity within the education system.

Sources: Benveniste 2000; Ravela 2005.

A.4. South Africa

Purpose. South Africa has conducted a series of national assessments at grades 3, 6, and 9. It also participated in three international studies (a) to provide baseline data against which future progress could be monitored and (b) to allow South Africa to compare curricula and achievement in mathematics and science with those in industrial countries. Each of the international studies could be considered a national assessment of educational achievement. Participation in international assessment provided an opportunity for capacity development.

South Africa was the only African participant in the Trends in International Mathematics and Science Study (TIMSS) in 1995, and it participated with Morocco and Tunisia in TIMSS in 1999, and with those countries and Botswana, Ghana, and Egypt in TIMSS in 2003. South Africa also participated in the Southern and Eastern Africa Consortium for Monitoring Educational Quality grade 6 assessment that was carried out in 2000 and in the grade 4 Monitoring Learning Achievement assessment, which commenced in 1992.

Frequency. TIMSS 1995, 1999, and 2003.

Grade. 8.

Instruments. Achievement tests; student, teacher, and principal questionnaires.

Achievements assessed. Mathematics and science.

Who did it? Human Sciences Research Council in 1995 and 1999, and University of Pretoria in 2003.

Sample or population. Sample. One intact grade 8 class was sampled in each selected school.

Analysis. The study compared student performance in mathematics and science with that of other countries in terms of average performance and performance at the 5th, 25th, 50th, 75th, and 95th percentiles. It also compared South Africa with other participating countries in terms of students' backgrounds and attitudes, curricula, teacher characteristics, classroom characteristics, and school contexts for learning and instruction. It included a comparison of mean performance scores over time.

Use of results. TIMSS results have been used in parliamentary debates.

Interesting points. South Africa has 11 official languages. Some words had to be translated into South African English, and some contexts had to be modified. A considerable amount of time was devoted to solving logistical problems that are attributable to the inadequacies of services, such as mail and telephone, which are taken for granted elsewhere. The national research team found deadlines imposed by TIMSS difficult to honor. The initial effort at sampling unearthed about 4,000 schools that were not in the national database. Transfer of assessment-related skills between the teams that carried out the three TIMSS assessments has been limited. Only one of the staff members from the first TIMSS assessment team participated in TIMSS 2003. Most students took the test written in a language other than their home language.

The second TIMSS study was used for a detailed, in-country study (Howie 2002). Findings included the following:

- Official class-size statistics were different (much larger) from those found in the nationally representative sample of participating schools, which suggests inaccurate reporting of school enrollment data.

- Some students were afraid that their performance on the tests would count toward their official school results. Some were afraid to ask for help. Many struggled with open-ended questions. Late arrival, absenteeism, and cheating during test administration caused additional problems.
- Many students had problems completing tests and questionnaires because of language difficulties. Many teachers lacked the language fluency to communicate effectively with pupils.
- Teachers spent a lot of time teaching material that should have been covered in earlier grades.
- Close to one-quarter of the teachers of grade 8 students were not qualified to teach mathematics and had no postsecondary qualification.
- Pupils whose home language was either English or Afrikaans scored significantly higher than pupils who spoke another African language at home.
- Less than 0.5 percent of students achieved the highest level of mathematics performance, compared to 10 percent of the international sample. The mean score (381) for the highest scoring of the nine provinces (Western Cape) was significantly lower than the international TIMSS mean score (487).
- Neither school nor class size was a significant predictor of mathematics achievement.

National assessments at grades 3, 6, and 9 requested by the Department of Education were carried out to get baseline data for future assessments and to suggest policy initiatives. Each of those assessments used questionnaire data, as well as achievement test data, to provide a basis for evaluating long-term efforts to improve access, quality, efficiency, and equity. Provincial comparisons produced evidence of strong regional differences in achievement. Overall performance levels were considered low. For example, mean percentage-correct scores as low as 38 percent were recorded for language, 27 percent for mathematics, and 41 percent for natural sciences in the grade 6 assessment. Separate grade 6 reports were prepared for each province as well as for one national report.

Sources: Howie 2000, 2002; Kanjee 2006; Reddy 2005, 2006.

A.5. Sri Lanka

Purpose. To assess the achievements of pupils who had completed grade 4 in 2003.

Frequency. Previous assessments had been carried out at grades 3 (1996) and 5 (1994, 1999). Further assessments have been carried out at grade 4 (2007) and grades 8 and 10 (2005).

Grade. 4

Achievements assessed. First language (Sinhala or Tamil), mathematics, and English.

Instruments. Achievement tests; questionnaires administered to school principals, sectional heads, class teachers, and parents (see table A.5.1).

Who did it? National Education Research and Evaluation Centre, located in the Faculty of Education, University of Colombo.

Sample or population. Sample designed to be representative of the national population of grade 4 students and of grade 4 populations in each of the nine provinces.

Analysis. Comparisons of achievement scores by school type, location, gender, and level of teacher training. Provinces and districts were rank-ordered in each subject area. Path analysis was used to analyze relationships between school, home background, and student factors, on the one hand, and student achievement, on the other hand.

Use of results. Results were used for analysis of the education sector to help develop a new strategy for government and donor support for education and are currently being used to establish benchmarks against which student achievement levels in each of the provinces are being monitored.

Interesting points. The Sri Lankan national assessment team selected a score of 80 percent as the cutoff point for determining "mastery."[1] The percentages of students who were considered to have "mastered" each

---

[1] This determination was apparently based on a cutoff point used by the United Nations Educational, Scientific, and Cultural Organization in earlier Monitoring Learning Achievement studies (UNESCO 1990).

TABLE A5.1

Background Data and Source in Sri Lankan National Assessment

Type of information	Questionnaire	Sections	Number of questions
School background	Principal	• General background • Teacher profile • School facilities • Financial status • Opinions	37
	Section head	• General background • School facilities • Teaching-learning-assessment procedures • Opinions	13
	Class teacher	• General background • Academic and profes-sional information • Classroom details • Opinions	41
Home	Parents	• General background • Home facilities • Socioeconomic status • Learning support • Opinions	51
	Students	• General background • Preschool education • Post-school activities • Opinions	26

Source: Perera and others 2004, table 3.7.

of the three subject areas tested were reported. The results suggest that the expected standard was set at an unrealistically high level. While on the basis of mean scores, the report of the assessment concluded that overall performance in the first language "seems to be of a satisfactory standard" (Perera and others 2004, 47), when performance is assessed on the basis of mastery level, a different picture emerges. Fewer than 40 percent of students achieved mastery in the local language and in mathematics, and fewer than 10 percent did so in English. Results showed wide disparities in achievement among provinces and districts

TABLE A.5.2

Percentage of Students Achieving Mastery in the First Language, by Province

Group	Rank	Province	Percentage achieving mastery	Target percentage
Above 50%	1	Western	53.5	80.0
26–50%	2	Southern	42.6	80.0
	3	North Western	42.2	80.0
	4	Sabaragamuwa	40.2	80.0
	5	North Central	35.6	80.0
	6	Uva	33.9	80.0
	7	Central	33.8	80.0
1–25%	8	Eastern	23.7	80.0
	9	Northern	22.7	80.0

Source: Perera and others 2004, table 4.14.

(table A.5.2). Subgroups with low achievement levels were identified. Separate reports were published for each of the country's nine provinces.

Source: Perera and others 2004.

A.6. Nepal

Purpose. The 2001 national assessment was carried out to determine the extent to which student achievements had changed over a four-year period during a time of major policy changes.

Frequency. Baseline data were obtained on grade 3 students in 1997. (Grade 5 was assessed in 1999.)

Grade. 3.

Achievements assessed. Mathematics, Nepali, and social studies.

Instruments. Achievement tests of mathematics, Nepali, and social studies that were administered to all sampled students. Questionnaires were administered to headmasters and teachers of the three targeted subject areas in each sampled school. Twenty-five percent of students and their parents were interviewed.

Who did it? Educational and Developmental Service Centre.

Sample or population. A sample of 171 schools.

Analysis. Test scores above 75 percent correct merited a "satisfactory" performance rating. Other analyses included reliability studies of each test and comparisons of mean scores for 1997 and 2001. Analysis of variance was used to compare mean score performances of students across regions, and multiple regression analysis was used to identify factors related to student achievement.

Use of results. Results were used to monitor changes in achievement from 1997 to 2001 and, in particular, to evaluate the effect of policy changes that included budgetary increase, new curricula, new textbooks and teaching materials, and new teacher centers and teacher training centers. Highest-performing regions were identified. In 2001, the difference between boys' and girls' mean scores was significant only in the case of mathematics; boys recorded the higher mean scores. Overall mean social studies scores were significantly higher in 2001 than in 1997.

Interesting points. The data helped identify curriculum areas where students appear to have had some difficulty. In mathematics, students generally were able to describe words in numbers and numbers in words, measure time and weight, add numbers in words up to four digits, and add decimal numbers. They tended to be unable to do word problems involving any of the four basic operations (addition, subtraction, multiplication, division). In Nepali, the average student tended to be able to read a simple story and to use some vocabulary but not read and correctly answer questions based on passages or questions that described a pictorial story.

Results of the assessment showed that many of the reforms appeared to have had little effect. More than 60 percent of teachers indicated that their classes were never supervised. They tended to receive relatively little in-service support. About one-third were untrained. Classroom instruction was deemed ineffective.

The report concluded that although many reforms clearly had taken place, it was probably too early to expect improvements in student achievement. The national assessment report also highlighted the relatively poor quality of home support for education. More than one-quarter of mothers were classified as illiterate, while fewer than 7 percent had completed education up to grade 5.

Source: Khaniya and Williams 2004.

A.7. Chile

Purpose. Chile's Sistema de Medición de la Calidad de la Educación (SIMCE) was originally designed to help guide parents in school selection. It now seeks (a) to provide feedback on the extent to which students are achieving the learning targets considered minimal by the Ministry of Education; (b) to provide feedback to parents, teachers, and authorities at municipal, regional, and central levels; and (c) to provide data for policy makers to guide allocation of resources in textbook and curriculum development and in in-service teacher education, especially in the neediest areas. It aims to improve the education system by installing procedures that stress evaluation, information, and incentives. It also serves to underline the Ministry of Education's commitment to improve both quality and equity within the education system.

Chile also runs a separate but related assessment system as a basis for rewarding excellence under the SNED (National System of Teacher Performance Assessment in Publicly Supported Schools) by providing incentives to teachers and schools to raise student achievement levels.

Frequency. Annual.

Grades. 4 and 8.

Achievements assessed. Spanish (reading and writing), mathematics, natural and social sciences.

Instruments. Pupils who complete achievement, self-concept, and perception tests. Questionnaires that were completed by principals, teachers, and parents (one year only).

Who did it? First administered in 1978 by an external agency, the Pontificia Universidad Católica de Chile, the SIMCE assessment is now administered by the Ministry of Education.

Sample or population. All (practically all) students in the relevant grades are assessed in Spanish and mathematics. Natural science, history, and geography tests are administered to 10 percent of students. Very small schools in inaccessible locations are excluded.

Analysis. Schools receive a ranking in comparison with other schools in the same socioeconomic category, as well as a national ranking. SIMCE identifies 900 schools that score in the lowest 10 percent in the mathematics and language tests within their provincial regions for which special resources are provided (P-900 program).

Use of results. SIMCE results are used extensively in policy discussions. SIMCE reports classroom results containing the average percentage of correct answers for each objective assessed, as well as the average number of correct answers over the entire test. At the beginning of the school year, SIMCE reports results nationally and also by school, location, and region. SIMCE manuals explain the results and how teachers and schools might use them to enhance student achievement. P-900 program schools receive support in the form of improved infrastructure; textbooks and classroom libraries; teaching material; and in-service, school-based workshops. Schools are removed from the P-900 program when their SIMCE scores exceed the 10 percent cutoff limit.

The SNED program uses SIMCE scores along with four other measures of school quality. Teachers in the best-performing schools within a region receive a cash award roughly equivalent to a monthly salary. In an effort to ensure equity, the ministry selects schools catering to similar socioeconomic groups that are classified in terms of urban or rural location and elementary or secondary school level. Although a range of factors is taken into account in calculating the index, school achievement accounts for almost two-thirds of the index score (table A.7.1). The weighting system is regularly modified to reflect policy priorities.

Interesting points. SIMCE uses an intensive public-relations campaign that includes brochures for parents and schools, posters for schools, videos for workshops, television programs, and press releases. Reports are distributed to principals, municipal leaders, school supervisors, and ministry officials. Parents also receive an individualized report for their school. Newspapers publish school-by-school results. Because

TABLE A.7.1

Index for Merit Awards for Schools in Chile, 1998–99

Factor	Percentage
Effectiveness (SIMCE scores in math and science)	37
Value added (average SIMCE gain in score)	28
Initiative	6
Improvement in work conditions	2
Equality of opportunity	22
Parent-teacher cooperation	5

Source: Delannoy 2000, table 1.5.

municipalities receive funding from the central government on a per student basis, they have a vested interest in the outcome; good SIMCE results tend to attract more students and hence more revenue.

Schools that have a large number of absentees on the date of testing do not receive results. Some schools overestimated the extent of student poverty to help increase their chances of qualifying for aid under the P-900 program. Teachers tend to be more concerned with their school's rank relative to similar schools than with the opportunity to use the results to promote in-school dialogue to help diagnose areas where students appear to have learning difficulties. Some teachers have been critical of the overly technical nature of the school reports. SIMCE devotes relatively little attention to data obtained in student, parent, and teacher questionnaires. Attitudes to learning and student values proved technically difficult to measure. The SNED program assumes that financial incentives will inspire teachers to make greater efforts to enhance student learning.

Sources: Arregui and McLauchlan 2005; Benveniste 2000; Himmel 1996, 1997; McMeekin 2000; Olivares 1996; Wolff 1998.

A.8. United States

Purpose. The National Assessment of Educational Progress (NAEP), which commenced in 1969, measures students' educational achievements and monitors changes in achievement at specified ages and grades. NAEP, often termed "The Nation's Report Card," also examines achievements of subpopulations defined by demographic characteristics and by specific background experiences. The sample in most states in NAEP is sufficiently large to allow inferences to be made about achievement in individual states.

Frequency. Assessments are carried out at least once every second year in mathematics and reading and less frequently in other curriculum areas.

Grades. 4, 8, and 12. Separate state-level assessments using NAEP tests are limited to grades 4 and 8.

Achievements assessed. Mathematics, reading, science, writing, the arts, civics, economics, geography, and U.S. history. New subject areas to be assessed: foreign language and world history.

Instruments. Achievement tests in reading, mathematics, science, writing, U.S. history, civics, economics, geography, and the arts. A student questionnaire (voluntary) at the end of the test booklet collects information on students' demographic characteristics, classroom experiences, and educational support. A teacher questionnaire focuses on teacher background, training, and instructional practices. A school questionnaire seeks information on school policies and characteristics. Background data on students with disabilities or English-language learners are provided by the teacher.

Who did it? A National Assessment Governing Board, appointed by the Secretary of Education, has overall responsibility for NAEP. The board consists of governors, state legislators, local and state school officials, educators, business representatives, and members of the general public. Various agencies have been contracted to carry out aspects of NAEP. Over the 2003–06 period, separate agencies have had responsibility for each of the following activities: item development, analysis, sampling and data collection, distribution and scoring, and Web site maintenance.

Sample or population. Samples of grade 4 and 8 students at the state level (public schools only) and grade 12 students at the national level. The sample size for each NAEP test is about 2,500 students in each state. A separate, long-term-trend study reports national-level results in mathematics and reading for age samples 9, 13, and 17 drawn from both public and private schools.

Analysis. Each student takes only a portion of the overall number of test items in a given content area. Data allow for group comparisons (for example, male and female students in an individual state). Item response modeling is used to estimate the measurement characteristics of each assessment question and to create a single scale to represent performance. Sampling weights are applied to reflect population characteristics. Scales are constructed that permit comparisons of assessments conducted in different years for common populations on related assessments. Quality-control measures are applied at each analytical stage. Percentages of students falling into each of three proficiency levels—"basic" (partial mastery of prerequisite knowledge), "proficient" (competent command of subject matter), and "advanced" (superior level performance)—are reported.

Use of results. Results are widely publicized. Political spokespersons and others have used NAEP results to highlight both positive and negative messages about the quality of the U.S. school system.

Interesting points. NAEP monitors trends in subgroup performance. Particular attention is given to the rates of progress of minority subgroups, notably increases in reading scores since 1971. Overall, reading and mathematics scores increased for fourth grade students, and the racial achievement gap narrowed. Generally, flat growth rates in reading achievement were recorded during a period when the number of Hispanic students (who traditionally have had difficulty mastering reading in English) doubled. The changing nature of the student population makes it difficult to establish whether efforts to improve pedagogy and curriculum are having an effect.

Sources: Johnson 1992; U.S. National Center for Education Statistics 2005, 2006.

A.9. Uganda

Purpose. The National Assessment of Progress in Education (NAPE), which was conducted in July 2005 in the second school term, was one in a series of national assessments in Uganda. The specific objectives of the assessment were the following:

• Determine the level of pupils' achievement in English literacy and numeracy.
• Examine relationships between achievement and pupils' gender and age, school location (urban, peri-urban, rural), and zones of the country.
• Examine patterns of achievement.
• Compare achievements of grade 3 and grade 6 pupils in 1999 and 2005.

Frequency. Uganda has carried out national assessments of educational achievement since 1996. Initially, pairs of subjects (literacy and numeracy; science and social studies) were assessed on a three-yearly basis. From 2003, the focus has been on literacy and numeracy, which are assessed annually.

Grades. 3 and 6.

Achievements assessed. English literacy and numeracy. Oral fluency in English is assessed every three years.

Instruments. Achievement tests in literacy and numeracy. Earlier national assessments used pupil, teacher, and principal questionnaires. Assessments that collect questionnaire data are administered every three years.

Who did it? Uganda National Examinations Board (UNEB).

Sample or population. Initially districts within each of the country's 14 zones were sampled. The sample size was increased to ensure a minimum of three schools within each district.

Analysis. Pupils' scores on each test were assigned to one of four levels: "advanced," "adequate," "basic," and "inadequate." Scores corresponding to levels were determined and set when tests were being constructed by panels of officials from the National Curriculum Development Centre, Primary Teachers' Colleges, Education Standards Agency, UNEB, and teaching professions. On the 50-item grade 3 English test, the following score ranges were used to define levels of performance: 38–50 "advanced," 20–37 "adequate," 15–19 "basic," and 0–14 "inadequate." The panels decided that the adequate level was to be considered the minimum "desired" level of proficiency. Fewer than 40 percent of grade 3 students attained the desired proficiency level in English (table A.9.1). Achievement test results were reported (in percentage terms) according to pupils' age, school location (urban or rural), geographical region, and zone.

Use of results. UNEB printed a poster for each grade 3 and 6 classroom in Uganda, listing curriculum areas where national-level student performance was considered adequate (for example, "We can count numbers," or "We can carry out addition and subtraction of numbers written in figures and symbols") and less than adequate (for example, "Help us to develop a wider vocabulary," or "Help us to carry out division of numbers correctly," or "Help us to solve word problems in math"). It has prepared a similar poster for teachers.

UNEB has plans to disseminate key lessons learned from the 2005 NAPE in the form of separate user-friendly reports of the implications of NAPE for teachers, head teachers, supervisors and inspectors, teacher educators, and policy makers. It is also designing a pilot initiative to use national assessment approaches to help improve classroom-based assessment.

Interesting points. The vast majority of students had to take the tests in their second language. Finding a commonly used language in which to give a test would be very difficult. More than one-quarter of primary schools could not be included in the national assessment, in part because of civil unrest in particular regions. UNEB found that schools

TABLE A.9.1

Percentages of Uganda Grade 3 Pupils Rated Proficient in English Literacy, 2005

Rating	Boys (%)	Girls (%)	All (%)
Proficient (advanced + adequate)	36.9	39.7	38.3
Below desired proficiency level (basic + inadequate)	63.1	60.3	61.7

Source: UNEB 2006, table 3.02.

occasionally inflated their enrollment data to increase their levels of resource allocation.

Many of the language items tested came under the general heading of "grammar" (50 percent for third grade and 30 percent for sixth grade). In general, students found test items difficult. Many students obtained relatively low scores (see figure A.9.1). Although the typical grade 3 student was expected to be about 8 to 9 years of age, the actual average age of the pupils who sat for the grade 3 test was 10.2 years; some were 11 years of age and older.

Substantial achievement differences were found by zonal area. A total of 87.5 percent of grade 6 students in the Kampala zone achieved the desired proficiency level in English literacy. The corresponding percentage for each of six other zones was less than 30. Performance on the grade 6 writing subtest revealed substantial differences between expected and actual levels of performance. Roughly half the students achieved the desired proficiency level in writing a story about a picture, one-quarter in writing a letter, and one-tenth in composing and writing a story. The technical report includes a sample of student letter writing

FIGURE A.9.1

Grade 6 Literacy Test Score Distribution in Uganda

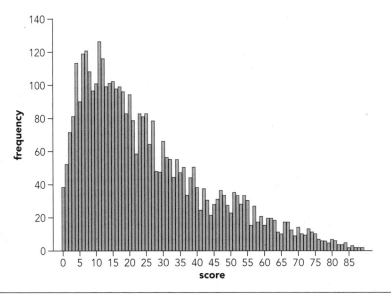

Source: Clarke 2005.

and lists of common mistakes in the mathematics tests. It also includes a series of recommendations and lists the agency or unit that should bear responsibility for following up on recommendations.

UNEB recruited the services of an external consultant to review the quality of its work, specifically the quality of the statistical characteristics of its items and the match between the selected items and curriculum objectives. The consultant noted a close match between the items and curriculum but recommended that more attention be devoted to problem solving in mathematics. The consultant's work was somewhat limited by the nonavailability of information on earlier national assessments relating to test development, sample weights, design, and analysis. Some of the problems stemmed from the fact that some NAPE analytical work had been contracted to a body outside UNEB. The consultant recommended that copies of all instruments, details of sampling analytical procedures, and other relevant documentation be kept on file by the national assessment agency (UNEB).

Source: UNEB 2006.

APPENDIX B

INTERNATIONAL STUDIES

B.1. TRENDS IN INTERNATIONAL MATHEMATICS AND SCIENCE STUDY

Framework

The central aims of the Trends in International Mathematics and Science Study (TIMSS) organized by the International Association for the Evaluation of Educational Achievement (IEA) were as follows:

- Assess student achievements in mathematics and science, described in terms of concepts, processes, skills, and attitudes.
- Describe the context in which student achievement develops, with a view to identifying factors related to student learning that might be manipulated through policy changes (relating, for example, to curricular emphasis, allocation of resources, or instructional practices).

Three TIMSS studies have been carried out: the first in 45 education systems in 1994–95 in three populations (grades 3 and 4; grades 7 and 8; last year of secondary school); the second in 38 education systems in 1999 in grade 8; and the third in grades 4 and 8 in 50 systems in 2003. Additional studies are scheduled for 2007, 2008 (last year of secondary school only), and 2011.

TIMSS distinguishes between the intended, the implemented, and the attained curriculum and, in analyses, explores how they are interrelated. The *intended curriculum* represents a statement of society's goals for teaching and learning that are typically described in curricula, syllabi, policy statements, and regulations and are reflected in textbooks, resources, and examinations. The *implemented curriculum* is how the intended curriculum is interpreted by teachers and is made available to students. Data on implementation (which provides an index of students' opportunity to learn) are collected mainly through questionnaires administered to teachers and students. The *attained curriculum* is what students have learned, as inferred from their performance on tests.

Instrumentation

The following mathematics components are assessed in TIMSS tests:

- *Content*. Numbers; measurement; geometry; proportionality; functions, relations, and equations; data, probability, statistics; elementary analysis; and validation and structure.
- *Performance expectations*. Knowing, using routine procedures, investigating and problem solving, mathematical reasoning, and communicating.
- *Perspectives*. Attitudes, careers, participation, increasing interest, and habits of mind.

The science components of TIMSS comprise the following:

- *Content*. Earth science; life sciences; physical sciences; science, technology, mathematics; history of science; environmental issues; nature of science; and science and other disciplines.
- *Performance expectations*. Understanding; theorizing, analyzing, solving problems; using tools, routine procedures, and science processes; investigating the natural world; and communication.
- *Perspectives*. Attitudes, careers, participation, increasing interest, safety, and habits of mind.

Since its inception, TIMSS has modified its frameworks to reflect curricular and pedagogical changes in participating countries. The

TIMSS designers used a curriculum framework that is based on earlier studies (in particular, the Second International Mathematics Study in the case of mathematics) to develop tests through a consensus-building process among participating countries. Several hundred items (multiple choice and constructed response) were piloted and evaluated for appropriateness and curriculum fit. Maximum curriculum coverage was attained without placing too great a burden on the students who took part in the study by distributing test items across booklets. Each student responded to only one booklet. Table B.1.1 presents an example from the curriculum framework for the TIMSS 2007 assessment.

Questionnaires were constructed and administered to obtain information on the following:

- General social and educational contexts (*system level*)
- Local, community, and school contexts (*school level*)
- Personal background factors (*individual student level*).

Instruments were translated into more than 30 languages.

TABLE B.1.1

Target Percentages of the TIMSS 2007 Mathematics Tests Devoted to Content and Cognitive Domains, Fourth and Eighth Grades

Fourth-Grade Content Domains	Percentages	
Number	50	
Geometric Shapes and Measures	35	
Data Display	15	
Eighth-Grade Content Domains	Percentages	
Number	30	
Algebra	30	
Geometry	20	
Data and Chance	20	
Cognitive Domains	Percentages	
	Fourth Grade	Eighth Grade
Knowing	40	35
Applying	40	40
Reasoning	20	25

Source: Mullis and others 2005, exhibit 2. Reproduced with permission.

Participants

Three populations participated in the original TIMSS in 1994–95:

- *Population 1*. Students in the pair of adjacent grades that contained the most students who were nine years of age (typically grades 3 and 4).
- *Population 2*. Students in the pair of adjacent grades that contained the most students who were 13 years of age (typically grades 7 and 8).
- *Population 3*. Students in the last year of secondary school. Two subpopulations were identified: (a) all students who took a mathematics and literacy test, and (b) students who were specializing in either mathematics or physics who took a specialized test.

In 1994–95, 45 education systems participated in TIMSS (Populations 1, 2, and 3). Among them, one was African (South Africa); six were in Asia/Middle East (Hong Kong, China; the Islamic Republic of Iran; Israel; Japan; the Republic of Korea; Kuwait; Singapore; and Thailand); and one was in Latin America and the Caribbean (Colombia). The names of education systems in this appendix are those listed in reports of the studies.

In 1999, 38 education systems participated in TIMSS (Population 2). Among them, three were in Africa (Morocco, South Africa, and Tunisia); 13 in Asia/Middle East (Chinese Taipei; Hong Kong, China; Indonesia; the Islamic Republic of Iran; Israel; Japan; Jordan; the Republic of Korea; Malaysia; the Philippines; Singapore; Thailand, and Turkey); and 2 in Latin America and the Caribbean (Argentina and Chile).

Fifty participated in TIMSS 2003 (Populations 1 and 2). Among them were 6 in Africa (Botswana; the Arab Republic of Egypt; Ghana; Morocco; South Africa; and Tunisia); 17 in Asia/Middle East (Bahrain; Chinese Taipei; Hong Kong, China; Indonesia; the Islamic Republic of Iran; Israel; Japan; Jordan; the Republic of Korea; Lebanon; Malaysia; Palestine; the Philippines; Saudi Arabia; Singapore; the Syrian Arab Republic; and the Republic of Yemen); and 1 in Latin America and the Caribbean (Chile).

Some Findings

Table B.1.2 presents results for the 2003 grade 8 mathematics test. Roughly one-third of the students in the highest-performing systems

TABLE B.1.2
TIMSS Distribution of Mathematics Achievement, Grade 8

Countries	Years of Schooling*	Average Age	Mathematics Achievements Distribution	Average Scale Score	Human Development index**
Singapore	8	14.3		605 (3.6) ◉	0.884
►► Korea, Rep. of	8	14.6		589 (2.2) ◉	0.879
† Hong Kong, SAR	8	14.4		586 (3.3) ◉	0.889
Chinese Taipei	8	14.2		585 (4.6) ◉	–
Japan	8	14.4		570 (2.1) ◉	0.932
Belgium (Flemish)	8	14.1		537 (2.8) ◉	0.937
† Netherlands	8	14.3		536 (3.8) ◉	0.938
Estonia	8	15.2		531 (3.0) ◉	0.833
Hungary	8	14.5		529 (3.2) ◉	0.837
Malaysia	8	14.3		508 (4.1) ◉	0.790
Latvia	8	15.0		508 (3.2) ◉	0.811
Russian Federation	7 or 8	14.2		508 (3.7) ◉	0.779
Slovak Republic	8	14.3		508 (3.3) ◉	0.836
Australia	8 or 9	13.9		505 (4.6) ◉	0.939
‡ United States	8	14.2		504 (3.3) ◉	0.937
¹ Lithuania	8	14.9		502 (2.5) ◉	0.824
Sweden	8	14.9		499 (2.6) ◉	0.941
¹ Scotland	9	13.7		498 (3.7) ◉	0.930
² Israel	8	14.0		496 (3.4) ◉	0.905
New Zealand	8.5 - 9.5	14.1		494 (5.3) ◉	0.917
Slovenia	7 or 8	13.8		493 (2.2) ◉	0.881
Italy	8	13.9		484 (3.2) ◉	0.916
Armenia	8	14.9		478 (3.0) ◉	0.729
¹ Serbia	8	14.9		477 (2.6) ◉	–
Bulgaria	8	14.9		476 (4.3) ◉	0.795
Romania	8	15.0		475 (4.8)	0.773
International Avg.	8	14.5		467 (0.5)	–
Norway	7	13.8		461 (2.5) ◉	0.944
Moldova, Rep.of	8	14.9		460 (4.0) ◉	0.700
Cyprus	8	13.8		459 (1.7) ◉	0.891
² Macedonia, Rep. of	8	14.6		435 (3.5) ◉	0.784
Lebanon	8	14.6		433 (3.1) ◉	0.752
Jordan	8	13.9		424 (4.1) ◉	0.743
Iran, Islamic Rep. of	8	14.4		411 (2.4) ◉	0.719
¹ Indonesia	8	14.5		411 (4.8) ◉	0.682
Tunisia	8	14.8		410 (2.2) ◉	0.740
Egypt	8	14.4		406 (3.5) ◉	0.648
Bahrain	8	14.1		401 (1.7) ◉	0.839
Palestinian Nat'l Auth.	8	14.1		390 (3.1) ◉	0.731
Chile	8	14.2		387 (3.3) ◉	0.831
¹ ‡ Morocco	8	15.2		387 (2.5) ◉	0.606
Philippines	8	14.8		378 (5.2) ◉	0.751
Botswana	8	15.1		366 (2.6) ◉	0.614
Saudi Arabia	8	14.1		332 (4.6) ◉	0.769
Ghana	8	15.5		276 (4.7) ◉	0.567
South Africa	8	15.1		264 (5.5) ◉	0.684
¶ England	9	14.3		498 (4.7) ◉	0.930
Benchmarking Participants					
Basque Country, Spain	8	14.1		487 (2.7) ◉	–
Indiana State, US	8	14.5		508 (5.2) ◉	–
Ontario Province, Can.	8	13.8		521 (3.1) ◉	–
Quebec Province, Can.	8	14.2		543 (3.0) ◉	–

0 100 200 300 400 500 600 700 800

— Percentiles of Performance —
5th   25th   35th   95th
95% Confidence Interval for Average (±2SE)

◉ Country average significantly higher than international average
◉ Country average significantly lower than international average

* Represents year of schooling counting from the first year of ISCED level 1.
** Taken from United Nations Development Programme's Human Development Report 2003, p. 237–240.
† Met guidelines for sample participation rates only after replacement schools were included (see Exhibit A.9).
‡ Nearly satisfied guidelines for sample participation rates only after replacement schools were included (see Exhibit A.9).
¶ Did not satisfy guidelines for sample participation rates (see Exhibit A.9).

1 National Desired Population does not cover all of International Desired Population (see Exhibit A.6).
2 National Defined Population covers less than 90% of International Desired Population (see Exhibit A.6).
►► Korea tested the same cohort of student as other countries, but later in 2003, at the beginning of the next school year.
( ) Standard errors appear in parentheses. Because results are rounded to the nearest whole number, some totals may appear inconsistent.
A dash (-) indicates comparable data are not available.

Source: Mullis and others 2004, exhibit 1.1. Reproduced with permission.

scored at the advanced benchmark level. In sharp contrast, 19 of the lowest-scoring systems recorded 1 percent or fewer students at this benchmark level. Singapore was ranked first at both fourth and eighth grade on the test. Some systems demonstrated significantly higher average achievement compared with their performances in 1995 and 1999, whereas others experienced significant score declines. The Republic of Korea; Hong Kong, China; Latvia; Lithuania; and the United States were among those that improved at grade 8.

Overall, gender differences in mathematics achievement were negligible. Girls, however, outperformed boys in some systems, while boys did better in other systems. A high level of parental education was associated with higher achievement scores in virtually all systems. At both fourth and eighth grades in the 2003 study, the number of books in the home correlated significantly with students' mathematics achievement.

The extent of coverage of the curriculum tested in TIMSS 2003 varied across systems. Teachers' reports on grade 8 students indicated that, on average, 95 percent had been taught number topics, 78 percent measurement topics, 69 percent geometry topics, 66 percent algebra topics, and 46 percent data topics. More than 80 percent of students were taught by teachers who had at least some professional training in mathematics. Textbooks were widely used as the foundation for teaching. Calculator usage, in contrast, varied greatly from system to system. Widespread use in grade 4 was permitted in only five systems. Schools that had few students living in economically disadvantaged homes scored on average 57 points higher in grade 8 and 47 points higher in grade 4 than schools in which more than half the students came from disadvantaged homes.

B.2. PROGRESS IN INTERNATIONAL READING LITERACY STUDY

Framework

IEA's 1991 Reading Literacy Study served as the basis for the definition of reading literacy in the Progress in International Reading Literacy

Study (PIRLS). For PIRLS (both 2001 and 2006), reading literacy was defined as

> ... the ability to understand and use those written language forms required by society, and/or valued by the individual. Young readers can construct meaning from a variety of texts. They read to learn, to participate in communities of readers, and for enjoyment (IEA 2000, 3).

The assessment framework for PIRLS comprises two major reading purposes crossed with four processes of comprehension. The *purposes* are the following:

- *Literary.* Reading for literary experience in which the reader engages with text to become involved in imagined events and characters, and to enjoy language itself.
- *Informational.* Reading to acquire and use information, in which the reader engages with aspects of the real world represented either in chronological texts (for example, when events are described in biographies, recipes, and instructions) or in nonchronological text, in which ideas are organized logically rather than chronologically (for example, in discussion or persuasion texts).

The *processes of comprehension* require students to do the following:

- *Focus on and retrieve explicitly stated information.* For example, look for specific ideas; find the topic sentence or main idea when explicitly stated.
- *Make straightforward inferences.* For example, infer that one event caused another; identify generalizations in the text.
- *Interpret and integrate ideas and information.* For example, discern the overall message or theme of a text; compare and contrast text information.
- *Examine and evaluate content, language, and textual elements.* Describe how the author devised a surprise ending; judge the completeness or clarity of information in the text.

PIRLS was carried out in 2001 and 2006.

Instruments

It was estimated that using "authentic" texts (that is, ones typical of those read by students in their everyday experiences) for each purpose (reading for literary experience and reading to acquire and use information) would require four hours of testing time. Because expecting any individual student to sit for more than one hour in a test situation did not seem reasonable, the assessment material was distributed across 10 booklets, only one of which was responded to by each individual student.

Students' ability in each of the four comprehension processes was assessed in questions that accompanied texts. Two formats were used: multiple choice and constructed response.

Information on students' attitudes to reading and on their reading habits was obtained in a questionnaire. Questionnaires were also administered to students' parents, teachers, and school principals to gather information about students' home and school experiences that were considered relevant to the development of reading literacy.

Participants

The target population for PIRLS was defined as the upper of the two adjacent grades with the most nine-year-olds. In most systems, this was the fourth grade.

Thirty-five education systems participated in PIRLS in 2001. They included one in Africa (Morocco); six in Asia/Middle East (Hong Kong, China; the Islamic Republic of Iran; Israel; Kuwait; Singapore; and Turkey); and three in Latin America and the Caribbean (Argentina, Belize, and Colombia) (Mullis and others 2003). Forty-one systems participated in PIRLS 2006. The number from Africa increased by one (with the addition of South Africa). The number of Asian/Middle Eastern countries increased by two (with the addition of Chinese Taipei, Indonesia, and Qatar but with Turkey dropping out). One Latin American and Caribbean system participated (Trinidad and Tobago joined, while the three that had participated in 2001 did not participate).

PIRLS is scheduled for administration again in 2011.

Some Findings

Four benchmarks were created on the basis of students' test scores. Those benchmarks were the *lower quarter benchmark*, defined as the 25th percentile (the point above which the top 75 percent of students scored); the *median benchmark*, defined as the 50th percentile; the *upper quarter benchmark*, defined as the 75th percentile; and the *top 10 percent benchmark*, defined as the 90th percentile. If reading achievement scores were distributed in the same way in each country, approximately 10 percent of students in each country would be ranked in the top benchmark. Table B.2.1 presents the results for participating countries. It shows, for example, that 24 percent of English students scored in the highest category and that 10 systems had fewer than 5 percent of students in this category.

Girls recorded significantly higher mean scores than boys in all systems. On the items that measured reading for informational purposes, students in Sweden, the Netherlands, and Bulgaria scored highest. Early literacy activities before commencing school, such as reading books and telling stories, were positively related to later reading performance. Higher reading achievement scores were obtained by the children of parents who had favorable attitudes to reading. Students who spoke the language used in the assessment at home tended to have higher scores than students who spoke other languages. Principals' responses indicated that reading was emphasized across systems more than any other curriculum area in grades 1 to 5.

Teachers, on average, said that they asked the majority of fourth graders to read aloud to the whole class daily. They made relatively little use of libraries, even though libraries tended to be available. On average, most teachers relied on their own assessments rather than on objective tests when monitoring student progress. Almost two out of every three students said that they read stories or novels at least once a week. Across all systems, students' attitudes to reading were positively related to reading achievement.

TABLE B.2.1
Percentages of Students Reaching PIRLS Benchmarks in Reading Achivement, Grade 4

Countries	Percentages of Students Reaching International Benchmarks	Top 10% Benchmark	Upper Quarter Benchmark	Median Benchmark	Lower Quarter Benchmark
** England		24 (1.6	45 (1.9)	72 (1.6)	90 (1.0)
Bulgaria		21 (1.3)	45 (1.9)	72 (1.9)	91 (1.1)
Sweden		20 (1.1)	47 (1.4)	80 (1.3)	96 (0.5)
* United States		19 (1.3)	41 (2.0)	68 (2.0)	89 (1.2)
New Zealand		17 (1.4)	35 (1.7)	62 (1.9)	84 (1.3)
¹ Canada (O.Q)		16 (1.0)	37 (1.3)	69 (1.3)	93 (0.6)
Singapore		15 (1.5)	35 (2.3)	64 (2.3)	85 (1.6)
* Netherlands		14 (1.0)	40 (1.7)	79 (1.5)	98 (0.5)
Italy		14 (1.0)	36 (1.3)	69 (1.5)	92 (0.8)
* Scotland		14 (1.1)	32 (1.8)	62 (1.8)	87 (1.1)
Hungary		13 (0.9)	36 (1.5)	71 (1.2)	94 (0.6)
¹ Lithuania		13 (1.4)	36 (1.7)	71 (1.7)	95 (0.6)
Latvia		12 (1.1)	36 (1.6)	73 (1.5)	96 (0.6)
Germany		12 (0.8)	34 (1.3)	69 (1.2)	93 (0.6)
² Israel		11 (0.8)	28 (1.2)	54 (1.4)	79 (1.1)
Romania		11 (1.3)	27 (2.0)	54 (2.1)	81 (1.7)
Czech Republic		10 (0.9)	32 (1.5)	68 (1.5)	93 (0.7)
² Greece		10 (0.8)	28 (2.0)	60 (2.2)	89 (1.2)
France		9 (0.9)	26 (1.2)	60 (1.4)	90 (0.9)
² Russian Federation		8 (1.0)	27 (2.1)	64 (2.3)	92 (1.6)
Slovak Republic		7 (1.0)	23 (1.4)	59 (1.7)	88 (1.1)
Iceland		7 (0.6)	23 (1.0)	53 (1.0)	85 (0.8)
Hong Kong, SAR		6 (0.7)	26 (1.7)	64 (1.9)	92 (1.1)
Norway		6 (0.9)	19 (1.2)	48 (1.4)	80 (1.4)
Cyprus		6 (0.8)	18 (1.3)	45 (1.6)	77 (1.4)
Slovenia		4 (0.5)	17 (1.0)	48 (1.2)	83 (0.9)
Moldova, Rep.of		4 (0.9)	15 (1.8)	42 (2.5)	79 (1.7)
Macedonia, Rep. of		3 (0.4)	10 (0.9)	28 (1.5)	55 (2.1)
Turkey		2 (0.3)	7 (0.9)	25 (1.6)	58 (1.7)
Argentina		2 (0.4)	5 (0.8)	17 (1.6)	46 (2.5)
Iran, Islamic Rep. of		1 (0.2)	4 (0.5)	16 (1.4)	42 (1.9)
Colombia		1 (0.4)	3 (0.8)	14 (1.5)	45 (2.4)
² Morocco		1 (0.9)	3 (1.4)	8 (2.1)	23 (3.0)
Kuwait		0 (0.1)	2 (0.4)	10 (1.1)	36 (2.0)
Belize		0 (0.2)	1 (0.4)	5 (0.6)	16 (1.3)
♦ Ontario (Canada)		19 (1.4)	40 (1.8)	70 (1.6)	92 (0.8)
♦ Quebec (Canada)		11 (1.0)	31 (1.8)	67 (2.0)	94 (0.8)

0   25   50   75   100

Percentage of students at or above Top 10% Benchmark
Percentage of students at or above Upper Quarter Benchmark
Percentage of students at or above Median Benchmark

Top 10% Benchmark (90th Percentile) = 615
Upper Quarter Benchmark (75th Percentile) = 570
Median Benchmark (50th Percentile) = 510
Lower Quarter Benchmark (25th Percentile) = 435

* Canada is represented by the provinces of Ontario and Quebec only. The international average does not include the results from these provinces separately.

† Met guidelines for sample participation rates only after replacement schools were included (see Exhibit A.7).

‡ Nearly satisfying guidelines for sample participation rates after replacement schools were included (see Exhibit A.7).

¶ National Desired Population does not cover all of International Desired Population. Because coverage falls below 65%, Canada is annotated Canada (O, Q) for the province of Ontario and Quebec only.

2a National Defined Population covers less than 95% of International Desired Population (see Exhibit A.4).

2b National Defined Population covers less than 80% of International Desired Population (see Exhibit A.4).

( ) Standard errors appear in parentheses. Because results are rounded to the nearest whole number, some totals may appear inconsistent.

Source: Mullis and others 2004, exhibit 1.1. Reproduced with permission.

B.3. PROGRAMME FOR INTERNATIONAL STUDENT ASSESSMENT

Framework

The Programme for International Student Assessment (PISA) assesses the knowledge and skills of 15-year-old students at three-year intervals under the auspices of the Organisation for Economic Co-operation and Development (OECD). PISA was developed to provide regular indicators of students' achievement near the end of compulsory schooling for the OECD International Indicators of Education Systems.

Students are assessed in three domains: reading, mathematics, and science. To date, three PISA assessments have been carried out. In 2000, reading was the major domain assessed, with mathematics and science as minor domains. In 2003, mathematics was the major domain; reading and science were minor domains. In 2006, science was the major domain; reading and mathematics were minor domains.

PISA is designed to be used by individual countries (a) to gauge the literacy skills of students in comparison with students in participating countries, (b) to establish benchmarks for educational improvement in terms of the performance of students in other countries, and (c) to assess their capacity to provide high levels of equity in educational opportunities and outcomes. PISA attempts to assess the extent to which students near the end of compulsory education have acquired some of the knowledge and skills that are essential for full participation in society.

Participants

In 2000, 32 countries participated in PISA. Two years later, 11 more countries took the PISA 2000 assessment tasks. No African country participated in the 2000 assessment. Asian/Middle Eastern participants included two OECD countries (Japan and the Republic of Korea) and five non-OECD "partner" countries (Hong Kong, China; Indonesia; Israel; Russian Federation; and Thailand). Systems in Latin America and the Caribbean included Mexico as well as the following non-OECD countries: Argentina, Brazil, Chile, and Peru. All 30 OECD member states and a further 11 "partner" systems took part in 2003.

Among the new partner systems, one was in Africa (Tunisia); one in Asia (Macao, China); and one in Latin America and the Caribbean (Uruguay). Three original partner systems (Argentina, Chile, and Peru) did not participate in the 2003 assessment. Turkey, an OECD country, participated for the first time in 2003. By 2006, the number of participating systems had risen to 57. Tunisia remained the only participating African systems. New partner systems in Asia/Middle East included Azerbaijan, Chinese Taipei, Jordan, Kyrgyzstan, and Qatar. Latin American systems that had participated in either the 2000 or the 2003 assessment took the 2006 PISA tests, as did one new partner systems (Colombia).

The population of interest is 15-year-old students. They are sampled at random across grade levels in participating schools.

Instruments

The Reading Literacy test assumes that students are technically able to read and attempts to assess their ability to understand and reflect on a wide range of written materials in different situations. Three dimensions are identified: the *content* or *structure* of texts (continuous, such as narrative and descriptive, and noncontinuous, such as tables, charts, and forms); the *processes* that need to be performed (retrieval, interpretation, reflection, and evaluation); and the *situation* in which knowledge and skills are drawn on or applied (personal, public, occupational, and educational).

The Mathematical Literacy test is concerned with the capacity of students to analyze, reason, and communicate ideas as they formulate, solve, and interpret mathematical problems in a variety of contexts. Three dimensions are distinguished in the mathematical framework: *content* (space and shape, change and relationships, quantity, and uncertainty); *competencies* (the reproduction cluster, the connections cluster, and the reflection cluster); and *situations* (personal, educational, or occupational, public, and scientific). Test items tend more toward "real life" situations than is normally the case in conventional achievement tests (see figure B.3.1)

The Scientific Literacy test assesses students' ability to draw appropriate conclusions from evidence and information given to

FIGURE B.3.1

Sample of PISA Mathematics Items

CARPENTER

A carpenter has 32 metres of timber and wants to make a border around a garden bed. He is considering the following designs for the garden bed.

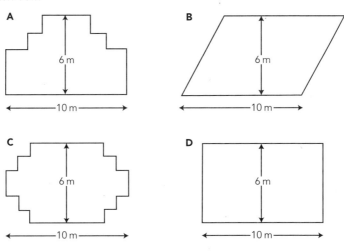

Question 1	
Circle either "Yes" or "No" for each design to indicate whether the garden bed can be made with 32 metres of timber	
Garden bed design	*Using this design, can the garden bed be made with 32 metres of timber?*
Design A	Yes / No
Design B	Yes / No
Design C	Yes / No
Design D	Yes / No

Source: OECD 2003. Reproduced with permission.

them, to criticize claims on the basis of evidence, and to distinguish opinion from evidence-based statements. The framework for science comprises three dimensions: scientific *concepts* (selected from physics, chemistry, biological science, and earth and space science);

processes (describing, explaining, and predicting scientific phenomena; understanding scientific investigation; and interpreting scientific evidence and conclusions); and *application* (in life and health; in earth and environment; in technology).

Having many more test items than an individual student could complete ensures adequate coverage of the domains of interest. Test items are spread across 13 booklets that consist of various combinations of mathematics, reading, science, and problem solving.

Questionnaires were administered to students (to obtain information on their engagement with learning, their learning strategies, and beliefs about themselves; their perception of the learning environment; and their home background) and to the principals of schools (to obtain information on school policies and practices and the quality of available resources) (OECD 2004b).

Some Findings

PISA reports the mean scores of countries in a "league table" (figure B.3.2). It also categorizes student performance by proficiency level based on what test scores indicate students can typically do. Figure B.3.3 describes the skills associated with each of six PISA proficiency levels for mathematics. The following figure (figure B.3.4) summarizes how students in each country performed by proficiency level.

The results indicate very considerable differences between countries such as Finland, the Republic of Korea, and Canada, where the majority of students score above Level 2, and Brazil, Tunisia, and Indonesia, where a small minority achieve this level of proficiency. Other findings show that less than 5 percent of students in OECD countries achieved Level 6, while about one-third were able to perform the tasks associated with Levels 4, 5, and 6. Eleven percent of students were not able to perform the Level 1 mathematics tasks. In most countries, males tended to score higher than females, especially in tasks associated with space and shape. In some countries (Australia, Austria, Japan, the Netherlands, Norway, and Poland), gender differences in achievement were not significant. Females tended to have a lower interest in—and enjoyment of—mathematics, and they claimed to experience more stress than males in this curriculum area. U.S. students tended to have

PISA Mean Reading Literacy Scores and Reading Subscale Scores, 2000

Combined reading literacy score

Country	Average
Finland	546
Canada	534
New Zealand	529
Australia	528
Ireland	527
Korea, Republic of	525
United Kingdom	523
Japan	522
Sweden	516
Austria	507
Belgium	507
Iceland	507
Norway	505
France	505
United States	504
Denmark	497
Switzerland	494
Spain	493
Italy	487
Czech Republic	492
Germany	484
Hungary	480
Poland	479
Greece	474
Portugal	470
Luxembourg	441
Mexico	422
OECD average	500

Non-OECD countries	
Liechtenstein	483
Russian Federation	462
Latvia	458
Brazil	396

READING SUBSCALES

Retrieving Information

Country	Average
Finland	556
Australia	536
New Zealand	535
Canada	530
Korea, Republic of	530
Japan	526
Ireland	524
United Kingdom	523
Sweden	516
France	515
Belgium	515
Austria	505
Norway	505
Iceland	502
Iceland	500
United States	499
Switzerland	498
Denmark	498
Italy	488
Spain	483
Germany	483
Czech Republic	481
Hungary	478
Poland	475
Portugal	455
Greece	450
Luxembourg	433
Mexico	402
OECD average	498

Non-OECD countries	
Liechtenstein	492
Latvia	451
Russian Federation	451
Brazil	365

Interpreting texts

Country	Average
Finland	555
Canada	532
Australia	527
Ireland	526
New Zealand	526
Korea, Republic of	525
Sweden	522
Japan	518
Iceland	514
United Kingdom	514
Belgium	512
Austria	508
France	506
Norway	505
United States	505
Czech Republic	500
Switzerland	496
Denmark	494
Spain	491
Italy	489
Germany	488
Poland	482
Hungary	490
Greece	475
Portugal	473
Luxembourg	446
Mexico	419
OECD average	501

Non-OECD countries	
Liechtenstein	484
Russian Federation	468
Latvia	459
Brazil	400

Reflecting on texts

Country	Average
Canada	542
United Kingdom	539
Ireland	533
Finland	533
Japan	530
New Zealand	529
Australia	526
Korea, Republic of	526
Austria	512
Sweden	510
United States	507
Norway	506
Spain	506
Iceland	501
Denmark	500
Belgium	497
France	496
Greece	495
Switzerland	488
Czech Republic	485
Italy	483
Hungary	481
Portugal	480
Germany	478
Poland	477
Mexico	446
Luxembourg	442
OECD average	502

Non-OECD countries	
Liechtenstein	468
Latvia	458
Russian Federation	455
Brazil	417

Legend:
- ☐ Average is significantly higher than the U.S. average
- ☐ Average is not significantly different from the U.S. average
- ▨ Average is significantly lower than the U.S. average

NOTE: Although the Netherlands participated in the Programme for International Student Assessment (PISA) in 2000, technical problems with its sample prevent its results from being discussed here. For information on the results for the Netherlands, see OECD (2001). The OECD average is the average of the national averages of 27 OECD countries. Because PISA is principally an OECD study, the results for non-OECD countries are displayed separately from those of the OECD countries and not included in the OECD average.

Source: OECD 2001, figure 3. Reproduced with permission.

FIGURE B.3.3

Student Proficiency Levels in PISA Mathematics

Score points	Level	What students can typically do
668	Level 6	At level 6 students can conceptualize, generalize, and utilize information based on their investigation and modeling of complex problem situations. They can link different information sources and representations and flexibly translate among them. Students at this level are capable of advanced mathematical thinking and reasoning. These students can apply insight and understanding along with a mastery of symbolic and formal mathematical operations and relationships to develop new approaches and strategies for dealing with novel situations. Students at this level can formulate and precisely communicate their actions and reflections regarding their findings, interpretations, arguments and the appropriateness of these to the original situations.
606	Level 5	At level 5 students can develop and work with models for complex situations, identifying constraints and specifying assumptions. They can select, compare, and evaluate appropriate problem-solving strategies for dealing with complex problems related to these models. Students at this level can work strategically using broad, well-developed thinking and reasoning skills, appropriately linked representations, symbolic and formal characterizations, and insight pertaining to these situations. They can reflect on their actions and formulate and communicate their interpretations and reasoning.
544	Level 4	At level 4 students can work effectively with explicit models for complex concrete situations that may involve constraints or call for making assumptions. They can select and integrate different representations, including symbolic ones, linking them directly to aspects of real-world situations. Students at this level can utilize well-developed skills and reason flexibly, with some insight, in these contexts. They can construct and communicate explanations and arguments based on their interpretations, arguments and actions.
482	Level 3	At level 3 students can execute clearly described procedures, including those that require sequential decisions. They can select and apply simple problem-solving strategies. Students at this level can interpret and use representations based on different information sources and reason directly from them. They can develop short communications reporting their interpretations, results and reasoning.
420	Level 2	At level 2 students can interpret and recognize situations in contexts that require no more than direct inference. They can extract relevant information from a single source and make use of a single representational mode. Students at this level can employ basic algorithms, formulae, procedures, or conventions. They are capable of direct reasoning and making literal interpretations of the results.
358	Level 1	At level 1 students can answer questions involving familiar contexts where all relevant information is present and the questions are clearly defined. They are able to identify information and to carry out routine procedures according to direct instructions in explicit situations. They can perform actions that are obvious and follow immediately from the given stimuli.

1 2 3 4 5 6 7 8 9 10 11 12 13 14 15 16 17 18 19 20 21 22 23 24 25 26 27 28 29 30 31 32 33 34 35 36 37

Source: OECD 2004a, figure 1. Reproduced with permission.

FIGURE B.3.4

Percentage of Students at Each Proficiency Level on PISA Mathematics Scale

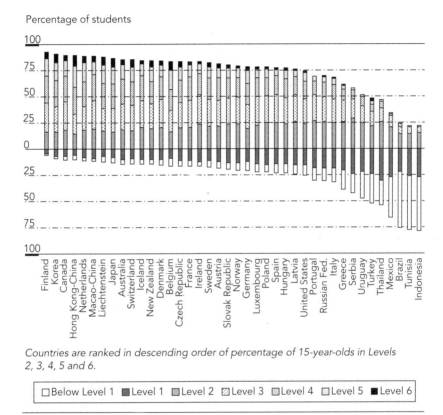

Countries are ranked in descending order of percentage of 15-year-olds in Levels 2, 3, 4, 5 and 6.

☐ Below Level 1   ■ Level 1   ■ Level 2   ▨ Level 3   ▨ Level 4   ☐ Level 5   ■ Level 6

Source: OECD 2003b, figure 2.16a. Reproduced with permission.

stronger "self-concepts" in mathematics than students in other countries. In contrast, students in Japan and the Republic of Korea, countries which had scored higher on the mathematics test, tended to have relatively weak self-concepts in mathematics. Parental occupation and parental support for education were strongly related to student achievement.

Gender differences in science achievement were seldom apparent. Similar percentages of males and females recorded particularly high and low scores. In reading, Finland's mean score was more than one-half a proficiency level above the OECD mean. Finland, along with the

FIGURE B.3.5

Percentage of Students at Each Proficiency Level on PISA Reading Scale

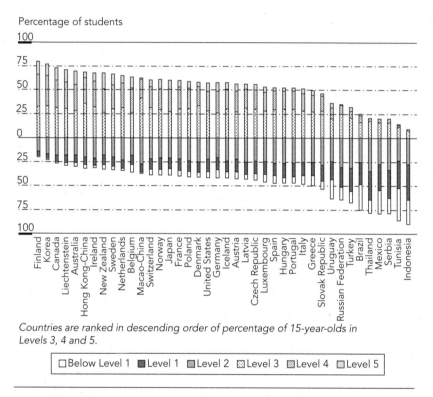

Percentage of students

Countries are ranked in descending order of percentage of 15-year-olds in
Levels 3, 4 and 5.

□ Below Level 1   ■ Level 1   ■ Level 2   ⊞ Level 3   ▨ Level 4   □ Level 5

Source: OECD 2004b, figure 6.2. Reproduced with permission.

Republic of Korea and Canada, also recorded relatively low internal
differences, suggesting greater levels of educational equity than in most
participating countries. Very few students in Indonesia, Tunisia, or
Serbia achieved at Level 3 or higher (see figure B.3.5).

APPENDIX C

REGIONAL STUDIES

C.1. SOUTHERN AND EASTERN AFRICA CONSORTIUM FOR MONITORING EDUCATIONAL QUALITY

Framework

The Southern and Eastern Africa Consortium for Monitoring Educational Quality (SACMEQ) is a voluntary grouping of ministries of education in southern and eastern Africa, comprising Botswana, Kenya, Lesotho, Malawi, Mauritius, Mozambique, Namibia, Seychelles, South Africa, Swaziland, Tanzania (mainland), Tanzania (Zanzibar), Uganda, Zambia, and Zimbabwe. Launched in 1995 with the assistance of the International Institute for Educational Planning (IIEP) of the United Nations Educational, Scientific, and Cultural Organization (UNESCO), SACMEQ was designed (a) to develop institutional capacity through joint training ("learning by doing" for education planners) and cooperative education policy research on schooling and quality of education (for example, identifying weaknesses in education systems in terms of inputs and processes) and (b) to monitor changes in achievement (IIEP 2007). A notable feature of SACMEQ is its systematic strategy for consulting with senior policy makers in government to identify issues of concern that might be addressed in empirical studies. It also seeks to promote stakeholder involvement and greater transparency in decision making. The first round of SACMEQ studies was carried out between 1995 and 1999.

Policy concerns for SACMEQ II studies that were carried out between 2000 and 2003 were clustered under five main themes (Murimba 2005b; Passos and others 2005):

- Pupil characteristics and their learning environments
- Teacher characteristics and perceptions (for example, on teaching and resources)
- School head characteristics and perceptions (for example, on the operation of schools and problems encountered)
- Equity in the allocation of human and material resources among regions and schools
- Achievements in reading and mathematics of pupils and their teachers.

SACMEQ was based on an earlier (1991) study carried out in Zimbabwe (Ross and Postlethwaite 1991) and began as a series of national studies. Nevertheless, it had an international dimension because studies shared many features (research questions, instruments, target populations, sampling procedures, and analyses). A separate report is prepared for each country. Cross-national comparisons were made for SACMEQ II but not for SACMEQ I.

Instruments

Data were collected on the reading literacy and numeracy levels of students in a test of achievement. A number of items from the Trends in International Mathematics and Science Study (TIMSS) were embedded in SACMEQ II tests to provide comparative data. Questionnaires were used to collect data on baseline indicators for educational inputs, general conditions of schooling, and equity assessments for human and material resource allocation. Information on home background conditions was obtained through pupil questionnaires; pupils were asked to indicate the number of possessions in their homes from a list that included items such as a daily newspaper, a weekly or a monthly magazine, a radio, a TV set, a telephone, a motorcycle, a bicycle, piped water, and electricity.

SACMEQ II tests included items selected from four earlier studies: the Zimbabwe Indicators of the Quality of Education Study, SACMEQ I, TIMSS, and the International Association for the Evaluation of Educational Achievement (IEA) Study of Reading Literacy. Using those items made possible the comparison of student performance in the studies with performance in SACMEQ II.

Reports devote considerable space to describing teacher characteristics (for example, qualifications) and conditions in schools (for example, classroom furniture, supplies, size, and space); how they compare with ministry benchmarks; and how they vary by school and location.

SACMEQ II adopted the definition of reading literacy used in the IEA Study of Reading Literacy (in 1990): "[T]he ability to understand and use those written language forms required by society and/or valued by the individual" (Elley 1992, 3). It also based the development of the test on the three domains identified in the IEA study:

- *Narrative prose*. Continuous text where the writer's aim is to tell a story, whether fact or fiction
- *Expository prose*. Continuous text designed to describe, explain, or otherwise convey factual information or opinion.
- *Documents*. Structured information displays presented in the form of charts, tables, maps, graphs, lists, or sets of instruction.

A table of specifications was constructed in which the three domains were crossed with seven levels of reading skill:

- Verbatim recall
- Paraphrase concept
- Find main idea
- Infer from text
- Locate information
- Locate and process
- Apply rules.

Mathematics literacy in SACMEQ II was defined as "the capacity to understand and apply mathematical procedures and make related judgments as an individual and as a member of the wider society" (Shabalala 2005, 76). The test assessed competency in three domains:

- *Number.* Operations and number line, square roots, rounding and place value, significant figures, fractions, percentages, ratio
- *Measurement.* Related to distance, length, area, capacity, money, time
- *Space-data.* Geometric shapes, charts, tables of data.

The table of specifications matched those three domains with five "proposed" (or expected) skill levels, ranging from, for example, the ability to undertake simple single operations using up to two-digit numbers (Level 1) to the ability to make computations involving several steps and a mixture of operations using fractions, decimals, and whole numbers (Level 5).

Most test items were in multiple-choice format.

Results were presented in three forms: (a) mean scores, (b) percentages of pupils reaching minimum and desirable levels of achievement, and (c) percentages of pupils reaching eight competence levels on the basis of an item response theory model scaling technique (Rasch).

Mean scores are average measures of performance and may be used to describe the performance of different categories of pupils (for example, boys and girls, pupils living in different provinces or districts).

Minimum and desirable levels of achievement were defined by expert committees (consisting of curriculum specialists, researchers, and experienced teachers) before the collection of data. Two levels were identified:

- A *minimum* level that would indicate a pupil would barely survive during the next year of schooling
- A *desirable* level that would indicate a pupil would be able to cope with the next year of schooling.

Analyses were carried out to identify the variety of levels of skills displayed by pupils and to provide greater insight into the nature of pupils' achievements. Reading skills associated with eight levels included the following:

- *Level 1.* Prereading: matches words and pictures involving concrete concepts and everyday objects.

- *Level 2*. Emergent reading: matches words and pictures involving prepositions and abstract concepts; uses cuing systems to interpret phrases by reading forward.
- *Level 3*. Basic reading: interprets meaning (by matching words and phrases completing a sentence) in a short and simple text.
- *Level 4*. Reading for meaning: reads forward and backward to link and interpret information located in various parts of a text.
- *Level 5*. Interpretive reading: reads forward and backward to combine and interpret information from various parts of a text in association with (recalled) external information that completes and contextualizes meaning.
- *Level 6*. Inferential reading: reads through longer (narrative, expository) texts to combine information from various parts of a text to infer the writer's purpose.
- *Level 7*. Analytical reading: locates information in longer (narrative, expository) texts to combine information to infer the writer's personal beliefs (value systems, prejudices, biases).
- *Level 8*. Critical reading: locates information in longer (narrative, expository) texts to infer and evaluate what the writer has assumed about both the topic and characteristics of the reader (for example, age, knowledge, personal beliefs, values).

Mathematics skills associated with eight levels included the following:

- *Level 1*. Prenumeracy: applies single-step identification or subtraction operations; recognizes simple shapes; matches numbers and pictures; counts in whole numbers.
- *Level 2*. Emergent numeracy: applies a two-step addition or subtraction operation involving carrying and checking (through basic estimation); estimates the length of familiar figures; recognizes common two-dimensional shapes.
- *Level 3*. Basic numeracy: translates graphical information into fractions; interprets place value of whole numbers up to a thousand; interprets simple common everyday units of measurement.
- *Level 4*. Beginning numeracy: uses multiple mathematical operations on whole numbers, fractions, decimals, or all of these.
- *Level 5*. Competent numeracy: solves multiple-operation problems involving everyday units of measurement, whole and mixed numbers, or all of these.

- *Level 6.* Mathematically skilled: solves multiple-operation problems involving fractions, ratios, and decimals; translates verbal and graphic representation information into symbolic, algebraic, and equation form.
- *Level 7.* Problem solving: extracts information from tables, charts, and visual and symbolic representations to identify and solve multistep problems.
- *Level 8.* Abstract problem solving: identifies the nature of an unstated mathematical problem embedded in verbal or graphic information, and translates it into algebraic or equation form to solve the problem.

Participants

Between 1995 and 1999, seven education ministries collected information in SACMEQ I on students' reading literacy in grade 6. Fourteen ministries completed SACMEQ II studies between 2000 and 2002 in a study of students' reading literacy and numeracy in grade 6. Conditions varied greatly from country to country. For example, gross national income was nearly 40 times more in the Seychelles (US$6,730) than in Malawi (US$170). Government expenditure on education varied between 30 percent in Swaziland and 7 percent in Tanzania, while the percentage of an age group enrolled in primary school ranged from about 40 percent in Mozambique to just over 90 percent in Mauritius, the Seychelles, and South Africa (Murimba 2005b).

Teachers, as well as pupils, took the achievement tests in a number of countries.

Some Findings

Considerable differences in achievement existed between countries (figure C.1.1). Only 1 percent of sixth graders in Malawi achieved the "desirable" level in reading, whereas in Zimbabwe the figure was 37 percent. Almost 4 in 10 pupils in participating countries in SACMEQ II reached the "minimum" level of mastery in reading (set by each country before the test was administered), but only 1 in 10 reached the "desirable" level.

FIGURE C.1.1

**Percentage of Grade 6 Students Reaching Proficiency
Levels in SACMEQ Reading, 1995–98**

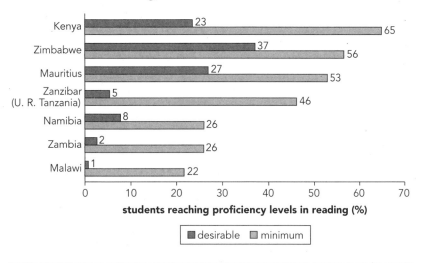

Source: UNESCO 2004, figure 3.1. Reproduced with permission.

Comparisons of the reading literacy scores of urban and rural students revealed large differences in favor of urban students in four countries (Kenya, Namibia, Tanzania, and Zambia), while in Mauritius and the Seychelles the difference was not statistically significant. The likely causes of urban-rural differences were complex. Compared to urban students, students in rural areas had lower levels of family socioeconomic status, were older, were more likely to have repeated a grade, and received less home support for their schoolwork. Furthermore, rural schools in general had fewer and lower-quality resources than urban schools, which was reflected in how teachers assigned and corrected student homework, how frequently they met with students' parents, and how much support was provided by inspectors (Zhang 2006).

An interesting feature of SACMEQ was the use of results to compare resource provision and trends in reading achievement over a time period that was marked by a rapid increase in school enrollment in the region. All six education systems that participated in SACMEQ I (1995) and

SACMEQ II (2000) registered an overall increase in resource provision in schools between the two assessments (Murimba 2005a). In five of the six countries, however, national mean literacy scores declined (figure C.1.2); those differences were statistically significant only in Malawi, Namibia, and Zambia. Overall, achievement scores declined on average 4 percent in the six countries.

Each national report produced a series of recommendations for policy makers. For example, the Tanzanian report recommended that the government investigate gender disparities in school enrollment and identify options to help eliminate the gender gap (Mrutu, Ponera, and Nkumbi 2005). This action would include providing care to orphaned children to relieve girls of heavy household responsibilities so that they could attend school.

A number of countries also assessed teacher subject mastery using the test that was administered to students. In Tanzania, fewer than half the teachers reached the highest level (Level 8) in reading (46.1 percent) or in mathematics (43.9 percent).

SACMEQ results have featured in presidential and national commissions (in Zimbabwe and Namibia), in prime ministerial and cabinet reviews of education policy (in Zanzibar), in national education

FIGURE C.1.2

Changes in Literacy Scores between SACMEQ I and SACMEQ II

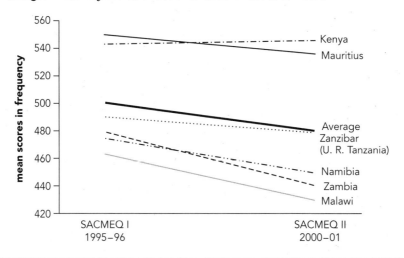

Source: UNESCO 2004, figure 2.4. Reproduced with permission.

sector studies (in Zambia), and in reviews of a national education master plan (in Mauritius).

In several countries, results were interpreted as indicating a need to provide standards for resources in education. For example, benchmarks for the provision of classroom facilities (such as desks per pupil and books per pupil) were introduced in Kenya. In Zimbabwe, special funds were provided for classroom supplies.

High dropout and low completion rates prompted the Ministry of Education in Kenya to strengthen its nonformal education sector to cater for those who do not fit into the formal system. Also in Kenya, SACMEQ findings on gender, regional disparities, and internal inefficiencies were used to guide the development of action plans to implement Education for All at national, provincial, and district levels (Murimba 2005a).

C.2. PROGRAMME D'ANALYSE DES SYSTÈMES ÉDUCATIFS DE LA CONFEMEN

Framework

The Programme d'Analyse des Systèmes Éducatifs de la CONFEMEN (Programme on the Analysis of Education Systems, or PASEC) is conducted under the auspices of the Conférence des Ministres de l'Éducation des Pays ayant le Français en Partage (Conference of Education Ministers of Francophone Countries across the World, or CONFEMEN). It was launched in 1991 at a conference of francophone education ministers in Djibouti, where the first study was carried out in 1992.

PASEC has as its primary objective to inform decision making in education and, more specifically, to address important national policy issues. It does so by assessing student achievement and by attempting to identify key factors associated with it, and their associated costs, in order to establish a hierarchy of potential educational interventions in terms of their efficiency.

Five features of PASEC are worth noting. First, it has an international dimension in which proposals for country studies are considered at a meeting of CONFEMEN member countries. If a proposal is approved, the national CONFEMEN representative becomes responsible for the establishment of an interdisciplinary group of experts within the ministry of education which, in turn, will become responsible for implementation (design of questionnaires, administration, data entry and analysis, preparation of report). PASEC, however, is not designed primarily to compare student achievement across countries.

Second, students are tested at the beginning and end of the academic year. This system means that in analyses, student entry characteristics can be taken into account to obtain a measure of student growth throughout the year.

Third, studies in four countries (Guinea, Mali, Niger, and Togo) were designed with a particular theme in mind. For example, Guinea and Togo took as their theme teacher employment policies (including teacher training) that had been introduced in Togo in 1983 and in Guinea in 1998 to reduce the cost of hiring more teachers while recognizing that those policies might affect the quality of education.

Fourth, beginning in 1995, the same instruments were used in five countries (Burkina Faso, Cameroon, Côte d'Ivoire, Senegal [1995/96], and Madagascar [1997/98]), allowing international comparisons to be made.

Fifth, in two countries (Côte d'Ivoire and Senegal), representative panels of students identified in grade 2 in 1995 were followed through to grade 6 in 2000 in longitudinal studies.

Instrumentation

Tests (with multiple choice and constructed responses) were constructed in French and mathematics on the basis of elements that were common to curricula in francophone countries in Africa. Tests were designed for administration at the beginning and end of grades 2 and 5. The end-of-year tests contained some items from the beginning-of-year tests in addition to items based on material covered during the course of the year.

At grade 2, the French tests assessed pupils' reading vocabulary, comprehension of sentences and texts, and writing. Grade 5 tests, in addition to assessing comprehension, assessed spelling and aspects of grammar.

The mathematics tests at grade 5 included items that assessed pupils' knowledge of the properties of numbers and their ability to carry out basic computations (addition and subtraction). Tests also included items that required pupils to use addition, subtraction, multiplication, and division in the solution of problems, as well as items that assessed pupils' knowledge of decimals and fractions and of basic geometric concepts.

In Mauritius, a test of Arabic and, in Madagascar, a test of Malagasy were also administered. In Cameroon, an English translation of the French test was administered to anglophone students.

Background data were collected in questionnaires administered to pupils on their personal (gender, age, nutrition, and language spoken) and their background (parents' education, availability of books in the home, and distance to school) factors and in questionnaires administered to teachers on their personal characteristics (gender, age, and education or training) and on their classroom environments.

In analyses, background factors were related to student achievement in an attempt to identify relationships between the two sets of variables. Particular attention was paid to "growth" or the "value added" during the course of a year and to the contribution of in-school factors, such as level of teacher training, class size, and textbook availability, as well as nonschool factors, such as parental education, distance to school, and home language (Bernard 1999; CONFEMEN 1999; Kulpoo and Coustère 1999).

Participants

To date, 18 countries have participated in PASEC activities: Benin, Burkina Faso, Cameroon, the Central African Republic, Chad, Côte d'Ivoire, the Democratic Republic of Congo, Djibouti, Gabon, Guinea, Madagascar, Mali, Mauritania, Mauritius, Niger, the Republic of Congo, Senegal, and Togo.

Some Findings

Results suggest low levels of achievement as reflected in reading and mathematics test scores (figure C.2.1). "Low achievement" was

FIGURE C.2.1

Percentage of Grade 5 Pupils with Low Achievement, PASEC, 1996–2001

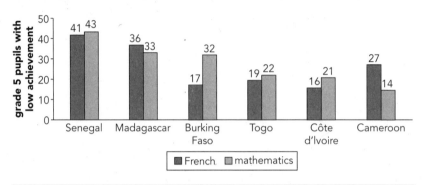

Source: UNESCO 2004, figure 3.32. Reproduced with permission.

Note: The assessment was carried out in Burkina Faso, Cameroon, Côte d'Ivoire, and Senegal in 1995/96; in Madagascar in 1997/98; and in Togo in 2000/01. Countries are ranked by proportion of low-achieving pupils in mathematics. Low achievement is defined as a score below the 25th percentile on reading and mathematics.

defined as a score below the 25th percentile on tests of reading and mathematics.

Several analyses of PASEC data have been carried out. In one of those, data from five countries (Burkina Faso, Cameroon, Côte d'Ivoire, Madagascar, and Senegal) were used in a hierarchical linear model to assess individual, school level, and national characteristics determining fifth-grade students' achievements in French and mathematics (Michaelowa 2001). The following were among the findings that emerged.

First, a variety of individual student and family characteristics (including parents' literacy and the use of French in the student's home) were related to student achievement. Second, although students might appear to benefit from grade repetition, gains were only temporary. Third, both teachers' initial education and regular in-service training appear important in determining student achievement. Fourth, the number of days teachers were absent from school negatively affected students' achievements. Fifth, even though they were paid less, "voluntary" teachers (employed by pupils' parents) were more effective than teachers who were civil servants.

Sixth, teacher union membership was significantly and negatively related to student achievement. Seventh, the availability of student textbooks had a strong positive effect on learning achievement. Eighth, class size (up to 62 students) was positively related to achievement. Ninth, learning in a multigrade classroom had a positive effect on achievement. Tenth, students in schools visited during the year by an inspector performed better than students in schools that did not have a visit. Finally, girls' achievement seemed to benefit from being taught by a female; boys' achievement seemed to benefit from being taught by a male.

C.3. LABORATORIO LATINOAMERICANO DE EVALUACIÓN DE LA CALIDAD DE LA EDUCACIÓN

Framework

The First International Comparative Study of Language and Mathematics in Latin America was carried out by the Laboratorio Latinoamericano de Evaluación de la Calidad de la Educación (Latin American Laboratory for Assessment of the Quality of Education, or LLECE). This network of national systems of education in Latin America and the Caribbean was created in 1994 and is coordinated by the UNESCO Regional Office for Latin America and the Caribbean.

The main aim of the study was to provide information on students' achievements and associated factors that would be useful in the formulation and execution of education policies within countries. It would do so by assessing the achievements of primary-school populations to address the following questions: What do students learn? At what levels does learning occur? What skills have students developed? When does the learning occur? Under what conditions does learning occur? (Casassus and others 1998).

A comparative framework was considered one of the best ways to increase understanding of the state of education within countries. The need for an international study in Latin America was indicated by the fact that few countries in the region had participated in such a study and, when they had, the studies had not taken account of curriculum features specific to the region.

Instruments

Achievement tests (two forms) in language and in mathematics—in which the curriculum content of each participating country was represented—were developed. Tests were multiple choice and open ended (in language only).

Language components included reading comprehension; metalinguistic practice; and production of text in Spanish, except in Brazil where students were tested in Portuguese.

Mathematics components included numbers, operations using natural numbers, common fractions, geometry, and measurement.

Extensive information was collected in questionnaires (completed by students, teachers, principals, and parents or guardians) on factors that were considered likely to be associated with student achievement (for example, school location and type, educational level of parents or guardians, and teachers' and students' perceptions of the availability of learning resources in the school).

Participants

In 1997, 13 countries participated in a survey: Argentina, Bolivia, Brazil, Chile, Colombia, Costa Rica, Cuba, the Dominican Republic, Honduras, Mexico, Paraguay, Peru, and República Bolivariana de Venezuela. Data for 11 countries are included in the first report of the survey.

In each country, samples of approximately 4,000 students in grade 3 (8- and 9-year-olds) and in grade 4 (9- and 10-year-olds) were assessed. The "oldest 20 percent of the total population" was excluded (Casassus and others 1998, 18).

Some Findings

Results, classified by type of school attended (public or private) and location (cities with population over 1 million, urban, and rural), indicate that Cuban students' achievement levels, regardless of school location, are far ahead of those in other countries (tables C.3.1 and C.3.2). More than 90 percent of Cuban students achieved

TABLE C.3.1

Percentage of Students Who Reached Each Performance Level in Language, by Type of School and Location, LLECE 1997

Country	Public			Private			Megacity			Urban			Rural		
	Level I	Level II	Level III	Level I	Level II	Level III	Level I	Level II	Level III	Level I	Level II	Level III	Level I	Level II	Level III
Argentina	95	77	57	99	93	78	96	85	72	96	79	59	88	62	42
Bolivia	87	55	30	91	70	46	90	66	39	87	58	35	77	40	24
Brazil	95	80	54	98	93	72	96	88	62	95	82	58	84	62	38
Chile	93	71	49	97	86	67	94	76	53	95	79	60	89	63	41
Colombia	89	59	35	97	81	56	96	79	53	89	60	36	89	57	33
Cuba	100	98	92	n.a.	n.a.	n.a.	100	99	93	100	98	92	100	98	92
Dominican Rep.	77	52	30	83	64	42	84	65	42	73	44	25	73	39	20
Honduras	87	55	29	94	73	44	92	67	38	87	55	29	78	35	17
Mexico	89	58	38	96	84	65	94	70	50	89	64	43	82	48	30
Paraguay	88	60	37	93	75	54	n.a.	n.a.	n.a.	90	67	44	81	51	32
Peru	86	55	29	94	78	54	92	70	43	85	57	34	71	30	13
Venezuela, R.B.de	88	59	38	91	70	49	91	68	48	88	60	38	84	58	39

Source: UNESCO 2001, table 8.
Note: n.a. = not applicable.

TABLE C.3.2

Percentage of Students Who Reached Each Performance Level in Mathematics, by Type of School and Location, LLECE 1997

Country	Public			Private			Megacity			Urban			Rural		
	Level I	Level II	Level III	Level I	Level II	Level III	Level I	Level II	Level III	Level I	Level II	Level III	Level I	Level II	Level III
Argentina	96	54	12	98	71	23	98	70	26	96	54	11	94	43	6
Bolivia	93	43	9	96	59	18	95	49	12	94	51	14	89	36	8
Brazil	93	52	12	97	67	26	96	58	17	94	55	15	84	40	7
Chile	92	46	7	97	57	15	94	49	10	95	52	12	87	38	6
Colombia	93	42	5	97	55	10	97	53	8	93	43	6	92	50	12
Cuba	100	92	79	n.a.	n.a.	n.a.	100	95	82	99	90	76	99	50	72
Dominican Rep.	82	37	4	86	43	7	86	42	6	81	36	4	79	38	7
Honduras	84	36	7	93	39	5	87	35	3	86	39	8	78	23	13
Mexico	94	55	10	98	69	20	97	62	13	94	58	13	90	46	10
Paraguay	87	29	2	90	49	12	n.a.	n.a.	n.a.	88	42	9	82	34	8
Peru	87	29	2	94	54	11	88	43	8	89	33	4	78	23	2
Venezuela .R.B.de	76	25	2	76	33	5	75	26	3	77	27	3	68	22	2

Source: UNESCO 2001, table 8.
Note: n.a. = not applicable.

the highest proficiency level (Level III) in language. With one exception (rural schools), more than 75 percent did so in mathematics. Whereas 72 percent of rural students in Cuba achieved Level III in mathematics, fewer than 10 percent of rural students did so in most of the remaining countries.

Further analyses of LLECE data focused on the extent to which the relationship between socioeconomic status (based on parental level of schooling and achievement) varied across countries (see figure C.3.1). The data indicate that socioeconomic gradients vary considerably among countries; the relationship is more pronounced in Argentina and Brazil than in Cuba, which had relatively little variation in level of parental education. Although students in private schools outperformed students in public schools, differences between the groups were not significant when student socioeconomic status was taken into account (Summit of Americas 2003).

FIGURE C.3.1

Socioeconomic Gradients for 11 Latin American Countries, LLECE

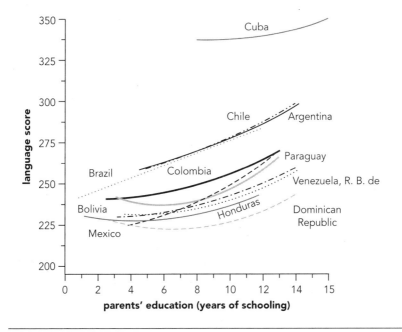

Source: Willms and Somers 2005.

Cuba had the least variation in parents' educational attainment, as well as the highest level of student achievement. Further analyses revealed that, in comparison with other countries, Cuba tended to have more day care, more home educational activities, smaller classes, more highly trained teachers, and fewer multigrade or ability-grouped classes (Willms and Somers 2001). In a follow-up study, LLECE results were used to identify schools with outstanding results in seven countries: Argentina, Bolivia, Chile, Colombia, Costa Rica, Cuba, and República Bolivariana de Venezuela (LLECE 2002).

Despite this variety of analyses, the Task Force on Education Reform in Central America (2000, 19) in its report titled *Tomorrow Is Too Late* noted that

> in almost every case there is no clear policy dictating how evaluation results can and should be used. Tests of academic achievement have not yet become a part of the accountability policies that are being demanded by various groups. There has been no discussion of the type of decisions that might be based on these results, and there is little consensus on the intrinsic value of assessing student performance. As a result, these programs are especially vulnerable to changes in government and even in senior ministry personnel.

REFERENCES

Arregui, P., and C. McLauchlan. 2005. "Utilization of Large-Scale Assessment Results in Latin America." Unpublished document prepared for the Partnership for Educational Revitalization in the Americas and the World Bank Institute.

Beaton, A. E., T. N. Postlethwaite, K. N. Ross, D. Spearritt, and R. M. Wolf. 1999. *The Benefits and Limitations of International Educational Achievement Studies*. Paris: UNESCO International Institute for Educational Planning.

Benveniste, L. 2000. "Student Assessment as a Political Construction: The Case of Uruguay." *Education Policy Analysis Archives* 8 (32): 1–41.

———. 2002. "The Political Structuration of Assessment: Negotiating State Power and Legitimacy." *Comparative Education Review* 46: 89–118.

Bernard, J.-M. 1999. "Les Enseignants du Primaire dan Cinq Pays du Programme d'Analyse des Systèmes Educatifs de la CONFEMEN: Le Rôle du Maître dans le Processus d'Acquisition des Elèves." Report of the Working Group on the Teaching Profession, Francophone Section, of the Association for the Development of Education in Africa (ADEA). Paris: ADEA.

Bhutan, Board of Examinations, Ministry of Education. 2004. *National Educational Assessment in Bhutan: A Benchmark of Student Achievement in Literacy and Numeracy at Class 6, 2003*. Thimphu, Bhutan: Ministry of Education.

Braun, H., and A. Kanjee. 2007. "Using Assessment to Improve Education in Developing Countries." In *Educating All Children: A Global Agenda*, ed. J. E. Cohen, D. E. Bloom, and M. B. Malin, 303–53. Cambridge, MA: MIT Press.

Campbell, J. R., D. L Kelly, I. V. S. Mullis, M. O. Martin, and M. Sainsbury. 2001. *Framework and Specifications for PIRLS Assessment 2001*. 2nd ed. Chestnut Hill, MA: Boston College.

Casassus, J., J. E. Froemel, J. C. Palafox, and S. Cusato. 1998. *First International Comparative Study of Language, Mathematics, and Associated Factors in Third and Fourth Grades*. Santiago, Chile: Latin American Laboratory for Evaluation of the Quality of Education.

Chinapah, V. 1997. *Handbook on Monitoring Learning Achievement: Towards Capacity Building*. Paris: United Nations Educational, Scientific, and Cultural Organization.

Clarke, M. 2005. *NAPE Technical Analysis and Recommendations*. Kampala: Uganda National Examinations Board.

CONFEMEN (Conférence des Ministres de l'Éducation des Pays ayant le Français en Partage). 1999. *Les Facteurs de l'Efficacité dans l'Enseignement Primaire: Les Resultats du Programme PASEC sur Neuf Pays d'Afrique et de l'Océan Indien*. Dakar: CONFEMEN.

Connecticut Department of Education. 2006. "State Releases Connecticut Mastery Test Results." News, August 9. http://www.sde.ct.gov/sde/lib/sde/PDF/PressRoom/2006cmtresults.pdf.

Coulombe, S., J.-F. Tremblay, and S. Marchand. 2004. *International Adult Literacy Survey: Literacy Scores, Human Capital, and Growth across Fourteen OECD Countries*. Ottawa: Statistics Canada.

Crespo, M., J. F. Soares, and A. de Mello e Souza. 2000. "The Brazilian National Evaluation System of Basic Education: Context, Process, and Impact." *Studies in Educational Evaluation* 26: 105–25.

Delannoy, F. 2000. *Education Reforms in Chile 1980–98: A Lesson in Pragmatism*. Washington, DC: World Bank.

Eivers, E., G. Shiel, R. Perkins, and J. Cosgrove. 2005. *The 2004 National Assessment of English Reading*. Dublin: Educational Research Centre.

Elley, W. B. 1992. *How in the World Do Students Read? IEA Study of Reading Literacy*. The Hague, Netherlands: International Association for the Evaluation of Educational Achievement.

————, ed. 1994. *The IEA Study of Reading Literacy: Achievement and Instruction in Thirty-Two School Systems*. Oxford, U.K.: Pergamon.

————. 2005. "How TIMSS-R Contributed to Education in Eighteen Developing Countries." *Prospects* 35 (2): 199–212.

Ethiopia, National Organisation for Examinations. 2005. *Second National Learning Assessment of Ethiopia*. Addis Ababa: National Organisation for Examinations.

Ferrer, G. 2006. *Educational Assessment Systems in Latin America: Current Practice and Future Challenges*. Washington, DC: Partnership for Educational Revitalization in the Americas.

Ghana, Ministry of Education, Youth, and Sports. 2004. *Results from Ghanaian Junior Secondary 2 Students' Participation in TIMSS 2003 in Mathematics and Science*. Accra: Ministry of Education, Youth, and Sports.

Greaney, V., and T. Kellaghan. 1996. *Monitoring the Learning Outcomes of Education Systems*. Washington, DC: World Bank.

Hanushek, E. A., and D. D. Kimko. 2000. "Schooling, Labor-Force Quality, and the Growth of Nations." *American Economic Review* 90 (5): 1184–208.

Hanushek, E. A., and L. Wössmann. 2007. *Education Quality and Economic Growth*. Washington, DC: World Bank.

Himmel, E. 1996. "National Assessment in Chile." In *National Assessments: Testing the System*, ed. P. Murphy, V. Greaney, M. E. Lockheed, and C. Rojas, 111–28. Washington, DC: World Bank.

————. 1997. "Impacto Social de los Sistemas de Evaluación del Rendimiento Escolar: El Caso de Chile." In *Evaluación y reforma educativa: Opciones de política*, ed. B. Álvarez H. and M. Ruiz-Casares, 125–57. Washington, DC: ABEL/PREAL/U.S. Agency for International Development.

Horn, R., L. Wolff, and E. Velez. 1992. "Educational Assessment Systems in Latin America: A Review of Issues and Recent Experience." *Major Project of Education in Latin America and the Caribbean Bulletin* 27: 7–27.

Howie, S. 2000. "TIMSS-R in South Africa: A Developing Country Perspective." Paper presented at American Educational Research Association annual meeting, New Orleans, April 24–28.

————. 2002. "English Proficiency and Contextual Factors Influencing Mathematics Achievement of Secondary School Pupils in South Africa." PhD thesis, University of Twente, the Netherlands.

Howie, S., and C. Hughes. 2000. "South Africa." In *The Impact of TIMSS on the Teaching and Learning of Mathematics and Science*, ed. D. Robitaille, A. Beaton, and T. Plomp, 139–45. Vancouver, BC: Pacific Educational Press.

Hoxby, C. E. 2002. "The Cost of Accountability." Working Paper 8855, National Board of Economic Research, Cambridge, MA.

Husén, T. 1973. "Foreword." In *Science Achievement in Nineteen Countries*, ed. L. C. Comber and J. P. Keeves, 13–24. New York: Wiley.

Husén, T., and T. N. Postlethwaite. 1996. "A Brief History of the International Association for the Evaluation of Educational Achievement (IEA)." *Assessment in Education* 3 (2): 129–41.

IEA (International Association for the Evaluation of Educational Achievement). 2000. *Framework and Specifications for PIRLS Assessment 2001*. Chestnut Hill, MA: International Study Center, Boston College.

IIEP (International Institute for Educational Planning). 2007. "Southern and Eastern Africa Consortium for Monitoring Educational Quality." IIEP, Paris. http://www.unesco.org/iiep/eng/networks/sacmeq/sacmeq.htm.

Ilon, L. 1996. "Considerations for Costing National Assessments." In *National Assessment: Testing the System*, ed. P. Murphy, V. Greaney, M. E. Lockheed, and C. Rojas, 69–88. Washington, DC: World Bank.

India, National Council of Educational Research and Training, Department of Educational Measurement and Evaluation. 2003. *Learning Achievement of Students at the End of Class V*. New Delhi: Department of Educational Measurement and Evaluation.

Ishino, T. 1995. "Japan." In *Performance Standards in Education: In Search of Quality*, 149–61. Paris: OECD.

Johnson, E. G. 1992. "The Design of the National Assessment of Educational Progress." *Journal of Educational Measurement* 29 (2): 95–110.

Jones, L. V. 2003. "National Assessment in the United States: The Evolution of a Nation's Report Card." In *International Handbook of Educational Evaluation*, ed. T. Kellaghan and D. L. Stufflebeam, 883–904. Dordrecht, Netherlands: Kluwer Academic.

Kanjee, A. 2006. "The State of National Assessments of Learner Achievement." Unpublished paper prepared for the Human Sciences Research Council, Pretoria, South Africa.

Keeves, J. P. 1995. "The Contribution of IEA Research to Australian Education." In *Reflections on Educational Achievement: Papers in Honour of*

T. *Neville Postlethwaite*, ed. W. Bos and R. H. Lehmann, 137–58. New York: Waxman.

Kellaghan, T. 1996. "IEA Studies and Educational Policy." *Assessment in Education* 3 (2): 143–60.

———. 1997. "Seguimiento de los resultados educativos nacionales." In *Evaluación y reforma educativa: Opciones de política*, ed. B. Álvarez H. and M. Ruiz-Casares, 23–65. Washington, DC: ABEL/PREAL/U.S. Agency for International Development.

———. 2003. "Local, National and International Levels of System Evaluation: Introduction." In *International Handbook of Educational Evaluation*, ed. T. Kellaghan and D. L. Stufflebeam, 873–82. Dordrecht, Netherlands: Kluwer Academic.

———. 2006. "What Monitoring Mechanisms Can Be Used for Cross-National (and National) Studies?" In *Cross-National Studies of the Quality of Education: Planning Their Design and Managing Their Impact*, ed. K. N. Ross and I. J. Genevois, 51–55. Paris: International Institute for Educational Planning.

Kellaghan, T., and V. Greaney. 2001a. "The Globalisation of Assessment in the 20th Century." *Assessment in Education* 8 (1): 87–102.

———. 2001b. *Using Assessment to Improve the Quality of Education*. Paris: International Institute for Educational Planning.

———. 2004. *Assessing Student Learning in Africa*. Washington, DC: World Bank.

Khaniya, T., and J. H. Williams. 2004. "Necessary but Not Sufficient: Challenges to (Implicit) Theories of Educational Change—Reform in Nepal's Education System." *International Journal of Educational Development* 24 (3): 315–28.

Kirsch, I. 2001. *The International Adult Literacy Study (IALS): Understanding What Was Measured*. Princeton, NJ: Educational Testing Service.

Kulpoo, D., and P. Coustère. 1999. "Developing National Capacities for Assessment and Monitoring through Effective Partnerships." In *Partnerships for Capacity Building and Quality Improvements in Education: Papers from the ADEA 1997 Biennial Meeting, Dakar*. Paris: Association for the Development of Education in Africa.

Lesotho, Examinations Council of Lesotho and National Curriculum Development Centre. 2006. *Lesotho: National Assessment of Educational*

Progress, 2004. Maseru: Examinations Council of Lesotho and National Curriculum Development Centre.

LLECE (Latin American Laboratory for Evaluation of the Quality of Education). 2002. *Qualitative Study of Schools with Outstanding Results in Seven Latin American Countries.* Santiago: LLECE.

Lockheed, M. E., and A. Harris. 2005. "Beneath Education Production Functions: The Case of Primary Education in Jamaica." *Peabody Journal of Education* 80 (1): 6–28.

Makuwa, D. 2005. *The SACMEQ II Project in Namibia: A Study of the Conditions of Schooling and Quality of Education.* Harare: Southern and Eastern Africa Consortium for Monitoring Educational Quality.

McMeekin, R. W. 2000. *Implementing School-Based Merit Awards: Chile's Experiences.* Washington, DC: World Bank.

Michaelowa, K. 2001. "Primary Education Quality in Francophone Sub-Saharan Africa: Determinants of Learning Achievement and Efficiency Considerations." *World Development* 29 (10): 1699–716.

Mrutu, A., G. Ponera, and E. Nkumbi. 2005. *The SACMEQ II Project in Tanzania: A Study of the Conditions of Schooling and the Quality of Education.* Harare: Southern and Eastern Africa Consortium for Monitoring Educational Quality.

Mullis, I. V. S., A. M. Kennedy, M. O. Martin, and M. Sainsbury. 2006. *PIRLS 2006: Assessment Framework and Specifications.* Chestnut Hill, MA: International Study Center, Boston College.

Mullis, I. V. S., M. O. Martin, E. J. Gonzalez, and S. J. Chrostowski. 2004. *TIMSS 2003 International Mathematics Report: Findings from IEA's Trends in International Mathematics and Science Study at the Fourth and Eighth Grades.* Chestnut Hill, MA: International Study Center, Boston College.

Mullis, I. V. S., M. O. Martin, E. J. Gonzalez, and A. M. Kennedy. 2003. *PIRLS 2001 International Report: IEA's Study of Reading Literacy Achievement in Primary Schools.* Chestnut Hill, MA: International Study Center, Boston College.

Mullis, I. V. S., M. O. Martin, G. J. Ruddock, C. Y. O'Sullivan, A. Arora, and E. Erberber. 2005. *TIMSS 2007 Assessment Frameworks.* Chestnut Hill, MA: International Study Center, Boston College.

Murimba, S. 2005a. "The Impact of the Southern and Eastern Africa Consortium for Monitoring Educational Quality (SACMEQ)." *Prospects* 35 (1): 91–108.

————. 2005b. "The Southern and Eastern Africa Consortium for Monitoring Educational Quality (SACMEQ): Mission Approach and Projects." *Prospects* 35 (1): 75–89.

Nassor, S., and K. A. Mohammed. 1998. *The Quality of Education: Some Policy Suggestions Based on a Survey of Schools—Zanzibar.* SACMEQ Policy Research 4, International Institute for Educational Planning, Paris.

Naumann, J. 2005. "TIMSS, PISA, PIRLS, and Low Educational Achievement in World Society." *Prospects* 35 (2): 229–48.

OECD (Organisation for Economic Co-operation and Development). 2001. *Outcomes of Learning: Results from the 2000 Program for International Student Assessment of 15-Year-Olds in Reading, Mathematics, and Science Literacy.* Paris: OECD. http://nces.ed.gov/pubs 2002/2002115.pdf.

————. 2003. *The PISA 2003 Assessment Framework: Reading, Mathematics, Science and Problem Solving Knowledge and Skills.* Paris: OECD.

————. 2004a. *First Results from PISA 2003: Executive Summary.* Paris: OECD. http://www.oecd.org/dataoecd/1/63/34002454.pdf.

————. 2004b. *Learning for Tomorrow's World: First Results from PISA 2003.* Paris: OECD.

————. 2007. "Sample Questions: PISA Mathematics with Marking Guide." OECD, Paris. http://pisa-sq.acer.edu.au.

OECD (Organisation for Economic Co-operation and Development) and UNESCO (United Nations Educational, Scientific, and Cultural Organization) Institute for Statistics. 2003. *Literacy Skills for the World of Tomorrow: Further Results from PISA 2000.* Paris and Montreal: OECD and UNESCO Institute for Statistics.

Olivares, J. 1996. "Sistema de Medición de la Calidad de la Educación de Chile: SIMCE, Algunos Problemas de la Medición." *Revista Iberoamericana de Educación* 10. http://www.rieoei.org/oeivirt/rie10a07.htm.

Passos, A., T. Nahara, F. Magaia, and C. Lauchande. 2005. *The SACMEQ II Project in Mozambique: A Study of the Conditions of Schooling and the Quality of Education.* Harare: Southern and Eastern Africa Consortium for Monitoring Educational Quality.

Perera, L., S. Wijetunge, W. A. de Silva, and A. A. Navaratne. 2004. *Achievement after Four Years of Schooling. National Assessment of Achievement of Grade Four Pupils in Sri Lanka: National Report.* Colombo: National Education Research and Evaluation Centre, University of Colombo.

Postlethwaite, T. N. 2004. "What Do International Assessment Studies Tell Us about the Quality of School Systems?" Background paper for *Education for All Global Monitoring Report 2005*, United Nations Educational, Scientific, and Cultural Organization, Paris.

Prakash, V., S. K. S. Gautam, and I. K. Bansal. 2000. *Student Achievement under MAS: Appraisal in Phase-II States*. New Delhi: National Council of Educational Research and Training.

Ramirez, F. O., X. Luo, E. Schofer, and J. W. Meyer. 2006. "Student Achievement and National Economic Growth." *American Journal of Education* 113 (1): 1–29.

Ravela, P. 2005. "A Formative Approach to National Assessments: The Case of Uruguay." *Prospects* 35 (1): 21–43.

Reddy, V. 2005. "Cross-National Achievement Studies: Learning from South Africa's Participation in the Trends in International Mathematics and Science Study." *Compare* 35 (1): 63–77.

———. 2006. *Mathematics and Science Achievement at South African Schools in TIMSS 2003*. Capetown, South Africa: Human Sciences Research Council Press.

Robitaille, D. F., A. E. Beaton, and T. Plomp, eds. 2000. *The Impact of TIMSS on the Teaching and Learning of Mathematics and Science*. Vancouver, BC: Pacific Educational Press.

Rojas, C., and J. M. Esquivel. 1998. "Los Sistemas de Medición del Logro Academico en Latino América." LCSHD Paper 25, Washington, DC: World Bank.

Ross, K. 1987. "Sample Design." *International Journal of Educational Research* 11 (1): 57–75.

Ross, K., and T. N. Postlethwaite. 1991. *Indicators of the Quality of Education: A Study of Zimbabwean Primary Schools*. Harare: Ministry of Education and Culture; Paris: International Institute for Educational Planning.

Shabalala, J. 2005. *The SACMEQ II Project in Swaziland: A Study of the Conditions of Schooling and the Quality of Education*. Harare: Southern and Eastern Africa Consortium for Monitoring Educational Quality.

Shukla, S., V. P. Garg, V. K. Jain, S. Rajput, and O. P. Arora. 1994. *Attainments of Primary School Children in Various States*. New Delhi: National Council of Educational Research and Training.

Sofroniou, N., and T. Kellaghan. 2004. "The Utility of Third International Mathematics and Science Study Scales in Predicting Students' State

Examination Performance." *Journal of Educational Measurement* 41 (4): 311–29.

Štraus, M. 2005. "International Comparisons of Student Achievement as Indicators for Educational Policy in Slovenia." *Prospects* 35 (2): 187–98.

Summit of Americas. 2003. *Regional Report: Achieving the Educational Goals*. Santiago: Ministry of Education, Chile; Paris: United Nations Educational, Scientific, and Cultural Organization.

Task Force on Education Reform in Central America. 2000. *Tomorrow Is Too Late*. http://thedialogue.org/publications/preal/tomorrow.pdf.

UNEB (Uganda National Examinations Board). 2006. *The Achievements of Primary School Pupils in Uganda in English Literacy and Numeracy*. Kampala: UNEB.

UNESCO (United Nations Educational, Scientific, and Cultural Organization). 1990. *Final Report of the World Congress on Education for All: Meeting Basic Learning Needs, Jomtien, Thailand*. Paris: UNESCO.

———. 2000. *The Dakar Framework for Action—Education for All: Meeting Our Collective Commitments*. Paris: UNESCO.

———. 2001. *Technical Report of the First International Comparative Study*. Santiago: Regional Office for Latin America and the Caribbean.

———. 2002. *EFA Global Monitoring Report 2002: Is the World on Track?* Paris: UNESCO.

———. 2004. *EFA Global Monitoring Report 2005: The Quality Imperative*. Paris: UNESCO.

U.S. National Center for Education Statistics. 2005. *National Assessment of Educational Progress: The Nation's Report Card, Reading 2005*. Washington, DC: U.S. National Center for Education Statistics.

———. 2006. "NAEP Overview." U.S. National Center for Education Statistics, Washington, DC. http://nces.ed.gov/nationsreportcard/about/.

———. n.d. "Comparing NAEP, TIMSS, and PISA in Mathematics and Science." U.S. National Center for Education Statistics, Washington, DC. http://nces.ed.gov/timss/pdf/naep_timss_pisa_comp.pdf.

Wilkins, J. L. M., M. Zembylas, and K. J. Travers. 2002. "Investigating Correlates of Mathematics and Science Literacy in the Final Year of Secondary School." In *Secondary Analysis of the TIMSS Data*, ed. D. F. Robitaille and A. E. Beaton, 291–316. Dordrecht, Netherlands: Kluwer Academic.

Willms, J. D., and M.-A. Somers. 2005. "Raising the Learning Bar in Latin America: Measuring Student Outcomes." Policy Brief, Canadian Research Institute for Social Policy, University of New Brunswick, Fredericton.

Winograd, P., and B. Thorstensen. 2004. "Using Large Scale Assessments to Inform the Policies and Practices That Support Student Learning." Working paper developed for the International Reading Association and the World Bank's Global National Assessment Training Project, Office of Education Accountability, Santa Fe, NM.

Wolff, L. 1998. "Educational Assessment in Latin-America: Current Progress and Future Challenges." Working Paper 11, Programa de Promoción de la Reforma Educativa en America Latina y el Caribe, Partnership for Educational Revitalization in the Americas, Washington, DC.

World Bank. 2004. *Vietnam: Reading and Mathematics Assessment Study.* Vols. 1–3. Washington, DC: World Bank.

———. 2007. EdStats database. http://www1.worldbank.org/education/edstats/.

World Declaration on Education for All. 1990. Adopted by the World Conference on Education for All, Meeting Basic Learning Needs, Jomtien, Thailand, March 5–9. New York: United Nations Educational, Scientific, and Cultural Organization. http://www.unesco.org/education/information/nfsunesco/pdf/JOMTIE_E.PDF.

Zhang, Y. 2006. "Urban-Rural Literacy Gaps in Sub-Saharan Africa: The Roles of Socioeconomic Status and School Quality." *Comparative Education Review* 50 (4): 581–602.

INDEX

Boxes, figures, and tables are indicated by "b," "f," and "t."